CHINA BASICS SERIES

A GLIMPSE OF THE CHINESE CULTURE

Authors: Feng Lingyu & Shi Weimin
Translator: Li Zhurun

2001.10

CHINA INTERCONTINENTAL PRESS

中国基本情况丛书

顾　　问　李　冰　赵少华

主　　编　郭长建

副 主 编　宋坚之(执行)　吴　伟

装帧设计　宁成春

本册责任编辑　冯凌宇

图书在版编目(CIP)数据

中国文化掠影／冯凌宇、史卫民著，－北京：五洲传播出版社，2001. 1

ISBN 7－80113－814－7

Ⅰ.中…

Ⅱ.①冯…②史…

Ⅲ.传统文化－中国－英文

Ⅳ. G12

五洲传播出版社出版发行

北京北三环中路31号　邮政编码 100088

HTTP：//WWW. CICC. ORG. CN

*

2001年3月第1版　2002年11月第2次印刷

889×1194毫米 32开 6.25 印张 55千字

004500

TABLE OF CONTENTS

Chinese Civilization — Origin and Development

The Chinese civilization dates to more than 5,000 years ago. Among the four greatest of all civilizations in the world, only the Chinese civilization has enjoyed an uninterrupted development. Erasable is the imprint of China's traditional culture in the souls of the Chinese — wherever they are, in China or outside.

Ever since remote antiquity, the Chinese nation has been a unified family comprising numerous ethnic groups. Time has changed the world beyond recognition - not the fundamental feature of China as a nation that is unified while diverse with a variety of ethnic groups and cultures.

The Chinese use a unique ideograph. Though the same words may be pronounced in various local dialects, the written language is the same and is good enough to ensure communication between people in all parts of China and enable people of today to read and appreciate records in classical literary style.

The Chinese people have had to their credit the "four great inventions" - paper, printing, compass and gunpowder which, along with porcelain and silk, once exerted a tremendous influence on the development of other cultures. The Silk Road, a web of land and sea routes in use for well over 1,000 years, bears witness to cultural exchanges between ancient China and countries to its west.

The traditional lunar calendar used by the Chinese is closely associated with crop farming in different seasons of the year. Traditional festival activities of the country's various ethnic groups are, in fact, bring to life those folkways they have been followed since ancient times.

Architectural structures in classical Chinese style are also

A classical style room on display at a Chinese cultural exhibition. Note the furniture, the porcelain jar under the table, the painting hung in the middle of the wall and the couplets at either side of it.

symbols of ancient Chinese civilization. Whatever they are — walled cities, palace complexes, religious shrines, residential buildings or gardens, these are imbued with a cultural spirit unique of the Chinese nation.

For well over 2,000 years, Confucianism has influenced the Chinese. In ancient China, the education and examination systems based on doctrines of Confucianism had a direct bearing on the operation of the feudal state power and development of the Chinese culture.

The Chinese people have created unique art forms of poetry, painting, music, dancing, and theatrical performance. Importance attached to ethical principles and love of Mother Nature are the essence of the Chinese literature and art.

Never have the Chinese people discriminated against alien religions. Instead, the Chinese have seen to it that different religions co-exist in harmony and peace on their soil. The Chinese culture

A colored pottery bowl excavated from the Banpo Ruins in Xi'an, Shaanx Prvince, which dates to 4, 800 BC-4,300 BC. Note the motifs of a human face with two fish.

has been able to constantly develop precisely because it is tolerant toward alien cultures and capable of assimilating them.

The Chinese use herbal medicine and acupuncture to treat diseases, and have developed numerous ways of preserving one's vital energy. The principles and methods of the traditional Chinese medicine to diagnose and treat diseases clearly demonstrate how the ancient Chinese saw Nature and how they handled relations between Man and Nature.

The Chinese people cherish special feelings for the legendary dragon and phoenix. These feelings, as a matter of fact, are an expression of their yearning for happiness and good luck by giving things in the natural world a cultural connotation.

Origin of the Chinese Civilization

China is one of the places where the human race originated. In China, remains related to almost all periods of Man's development have been found.

More than 200 sites of the Old Stone Age culture have been identified in all parts of the country. The Yuanmou Man, believed to have lived in what is now Yuanmou County of Yunnan Province some 1.7 million years ago, is the earliest species of *homo erectus* known to have existed in China. The discovery in 1929 of a skull of the Peking Man caused no small a sensation in the archeological community of the world. The Peking Man is believed to lead a communal life in caves some 700,000 to 200,000 years ago, and be using crude stone tools for a living on foraging and hunting. In a cave the Peking Man lived in, archeologists have found four stacks of ash along with rocks and animal bones with cracks that were obviously caused by burning. These are evidences to the fact that the Peking Man already knew how to use natural fire and preserve cinders.

The New Stone Age began in China around 8,000 years ago, when ancestors of the Chinese people became able to make stone tools by grinding and polishing, cultivate crops and domesticate animals. This suggests that foraging and hunting ceased to be their sole means of survival. As time went by, people stopped roving and came to settle down for crop farming as the chief means of subsistence. Natural conditions are favorable to crop farming in vast areas of China, and the most fertile parts of the land, the Yellow River and Yangtze River valleys, were the best developed in the New Stone Age. The Yellow River Valley became the earliest producer of broomcorn and foxtail millet, and it is in the Yangtze River Valley that rice farming originated. Remains of a primitive agricultural culture have also been found in areas drained by the Liaohe River in the northeast, as well as in parts of China's deep south.

A matriarchal clan society featured the early phase of the New Stone Age. The Yangshao Culture,[1] which dates to 5,000 to 3,000 years BC, was the best representative of the matriarchal clan

Pottery jars excavated from the Majiayao Ruins in Lintao County, Gansu Province, which date to 3,300 BC-2,900 BC.

society during its heydays. The Yangshao Culture falls into several types dating to different periods. One is represented by the Banpo Ruins in Xi'an City, Shaanxi Province. Excavations done so far on the ruins there prove that the Banpo residents were able to build residential buildings. They led a settled life in villages of fairly large sizes, used pottery containers to cook food or hold things with, and made pottery swords for cutting. In one of the pottery jars excavated from the Banpo Ruins, archaeologists found cabbage, leaf mustard and other seeds. Many pottery vessels are painted in red with brown or black motifs in shapes of human figures or fish, and for this, they are referred to as *cai tao* or "painted pottery". Also unearthed in Banpo are spinning wheels, suggesting that primitive residents there were already producing and using linen textiles.

The Amudu Culture on the lower reaches of the Yangtze River dates to 5,000 BC to 4,000 BC. Its discovery at Amudu Village, Yuyao County, Zhejiang Province, east China, is equally important to studies of the New Stone Age in China. Pottery ware unearthed here — bowls, plates, basins, jars, etc. — are black in color and in shapes that are rarely seen in pottery artifacts belonging to other primitive cultures identified in China. A wealth of stone, bone and wooden articles for daily use were also unearthed. Among these, structural parts of looms, textile pieces made of plant fibers, painted wooden bowls and ivory carvings testify to how developed primitive production techniques and handcraft skills had become. What merit special attention are the remains of wooden columns and platforms for raised pile dwellings and water wells. Also found are remains of long-grained glutinous rice seeds, bones of pigs, dogs, buffaloes and other domestic animals and a variety of fruit, suggesting that the primitive Amudu residents led a settled life, and engaged in production of rice and other crops while undertaking forage and hunting as sidelines. The discovery and identification of the Amudu Culture prove that like the Yellow River Valley, the Yangtze River Valley was a cradle of the Chinese

Jade ornament *cong* excavated from the Liangzhu Ruins in Yuhang County, Zhejiang Province, which dates to 3,300 BC-2,200 BC.

culture.

About 5,000 years ago, China entered the patriarchal clan society. In the Yellow River Valley, a typical example of this patriarchal clan society was the Longshan Culture (from 2,500 years BC to 2,000 years BC) found in Shandong Province. In the Yangtze River Valley, there grew the Liangzhu Culture (from 3, 300 years BC to 2,200 years BC), which was also found in Zhejiang Province. Pottery and jade artifacts of the Liangzhu Culture indicate that division between some branches of handicrafts industry and agriculture had, by and large, been completed. Moreover, excavation of graves brings to light that in the mid- and late period of the Liangzhu Culture, people were already divided into the rich and the poor, and those who were high in social status and those who were low. From some large graves archeologists unearthed *cong* (long hollow pieces of jade with rectangular sides) that symbolized the divine power, jade *yue* (battle axes) that symbolized military power, as well as large numbers of jade *bi*.[2] In contrast, only a few simple pottery vessels or stone tools are found in smaller graves, and there are also graves without burial objects at all.

Clay head of a pre-history goddess excavated from the Niuheliang Ruins in Liaoning Province. Note its eyes, which are inlaid with jade pieces.

Earthen burial mounds, altars and divine emblems of jade identified as belonging to the Liangzhu Culture suggest that a combination of divine and monarchical powers was emerging, which was to become the most salient feature of feudal China in the milleniums to come.

The Hongshan Culture (about 3,500 years BC) on the outskirts of Chifeng City, Inner Mongolia Autonomous Region, is unique among those primitive cultures found so far in China. It is quite different from cultures of *zhongyuan* (central China region on the middle and lower reaches of the Yellow River that encompasses most parts of what is now Henan Province, the western part of Shandong and the southern parts of Shanxi and Hebei). Highly developed as it was, the Hongshan Culture is however shrouded in mystery. A large altar, a fairy temple and a tomb of piled up rocks are the most salient features of the Hongshan Culture. These are in an area of 50 square kilometers, forming a huge sacrificial center — so huge that it dwarfs any of the primitive clan villages found anywhere in the country. Archeologists conclude that there should be something still larger surrounding the site, and that the Hongshan Culture should represent a fully developed society. No traces of human inhabitation were found at the site, but the discovery provides ample information to indicate that a new society was in the making — something that served as the social background for the existence of the Hongshan Culture.

From the northeast to the Pearl River Valley in China's deep south, archeologists have found numerous "local cultures" that are obviously independent of one another in origin and other features. Like the Hongshan Culture, these "local cultures" existed side by side with the cultures of the central China region, the mainstream of the primitive Chinese cultures. As Professor Su Bingqi, a prestigious archeologist, rightly puts it, "the origin of the Chinese culture should be compared to stars that stud the sky, not to a single candle." "The different ethnic groups that form the Chinese nation may have entered civilized society at different times, not simultaneously. Yet all took part in the building of the Chinese civilization by contributing to it what is the best in them."

Extension and Development of the Chinese Civilization

In about 21st century BC, the Xia, China's first monarchical power, came into being in the western part of what is now Henan Province and the southern part of what is now Shanxi Province. The dynasty reigned until the 16th century BC. There is plenty of documentation about Xia in classical history works - for example, about how the Xia people built water control projects to protect crops from being flooded and how they worked out a calendar for farm work in different seasons of the year. Over the past decades, archeologists have found remains they believe to date to the Xia period, and the finds invariably conform to the chronicles of the dynasty and the records of the administrative division for the dynasty's territory. Ancient records about

This square-shaped bronze *ding*, a food container, dates to the Shang period (16th century BC-11th century BC). It was indispensable at sacrificial ceremonies and banquets.

A bronze human head belonging to the mid-Shang period (16ᵗʰ century BC-11ᵗʰ century BC), which was excavated from the Sanxingdui Ruins in Guanghan County, Sichuan Province. It is a masterpiece of the Bashu culture, a branch of the Chinese culture that originates in the Sichuan Basin.

the history of Xia are thus confirmed. Nevertheless, archeological finds that are significant enough to serve as landmarks of the Xia civilization are still too few to be convincing. Moreover, remains of large Xia cities are yet to be found, and so are philosophical records left over from the dynasty itself.

The succeeding Shang Dynasty (about 16th century BC-11th century BC), however, left over sufficient philological records about itself. The dynasty came into being in the northern part of the Yellow River Valley, and had moved its capital several times before it settled in Yin or what is now Anyang of Henan Province. In Anyang, archeologists have found the foundations of scores of Shang Dynasty temples and palaces as well as tombs of Shang rulers, the foundations suggesting that the buildings were in neat clusters. What merit special mention are those ideographs cut on tortoise shells or animal bones unearthed from the Yin ruins. These oracle bone inscriptions, known as *jiaguwen,* are in fact Chinese characters in the most primitive form known to us. A large part of the inscriptions have been identified and this, in itself, serves as a convincing proof to the consistence of the Chinese civilization in all stages of its development.

Many oracle bone inscriptions are actually records of events related to agriculture, for example, records of sacrificial rituals to beg the Heaven for good harvests or rain, suggesting that the Shang rulers attached much importance to agricultural production and, consequently, to changes in weather as well. Food grain was no longer meant solely for eating, and people were able to turn them into alcoholic drinks. Moreover, people of the Shang period were raising silkworm cocoons and able to weave fine filaments of cocoons into textiles for clothing. Bronze smelting techniques of the Shang period were fairly sophisticated. Meat, grain and wine vessels used by Shang rulers at sacrificial rituals were all made of bronze. In the Shang and succeeding dynasties, there was a widespread use of bronze vessels — in court ceremonies, banquets and burials, etc. In other words, bronze vessels were no longer used just as containers. They symbolized the powers and positions of their owners as well. This is a most important distinguishing feature of ancient Chinese bronze vessels, relative to those found in other countries.

The Zhou Dynasty (11th century BC-256 BC) succeeded the Shang. Under the political system of enfeoffment, the supreme ruler, *tian zi* (son of the Heaven), conferred the title "prince" or "duke" on their relatives and favorite officials, and invested territories with them along with the people bound to the territories. Dukes and princes had the duty to make obeisance to the "son of the Heaven" and pay tributes to him regularly, and they also had the obligation to protect the sovereign. This system was patriarchal. The titles of *tian zi*, duke and prince were to be handed down to the eldest sons in the families' direct line of descent, while the other sons were invested with fiefs under titles of duke, prince, *qing, daifu* or *shi* in descending order of status. The system of enfeoffment was abolished later, but the patriarchal ideas that originated from it were to exert a strong influence on China's feudal society of more than 2,000 years.

In 771 BC, a nomadic tribe from the northwest seized the Zhou capital. In the following year, the Zhou rulers moved from the west bank of the Yellow River to the east bank, where they continued to reign supreme. For this reason, the Zhou Dynasty before 771 BC is referred to as the "West Zhou" and the Zhou

Dynasty after 771 BC, as the "East Zhou". By tradition, the East Zhou is divided into two periods: the Spring and Autumn period (770 BC-476 BC) and the Warring States period (475 BC-221 BC) period.

The East Zhou existed for a long time, but never were the "heavenly sons" able to consolidate their power. The various dukedoms or states just ignored their "common sovereign" and kept fighting one another for supremacy. Despite the chaos caused by incessant wars, use of iron tools and farm cattle and construction of water control facilities significantly improved agricultural productivity. Commerce thrived as cities kept springing up and copper coins were put into circulation. Increasing numbers of peasants became slaves of merchants or shifted to commerce, prompting many dukedoms or states to practice policies that aimed at encouraging agricultural production while restricting the development of commerce.

China experienced a cultural boom as well even though the political situation was chaotic. Monopoly of education by the nobility was broken, and scholars from among commoners traveled from one state or dukedom to another for chances to have their ideas adopted by the rulers. This state of affairs became even more spectacular during the Warring States period, in which dramatic social changes took place. Scholars representing the interests of different social groups busied themselves writing scholarly works and giving lectures to disseminate their philosophies and ideas of ethics and their theories of government. Different schools of thought were developed through contention in this historic period that was full of vitality and creativeness. The theories and thoughts of philosophy, political and military sciences, literature and art advanced by the exponents of the various schools of thought formed the basis for the development of the Chinese culture and scholarly learning over the next 2,000 years. With support of all imperial dynasties that followed the Qin (221 BC-207 BC), Confucianism founded by Confucius became feudal China's orthodox philosophy and ideology.

In 221 BC, the State of Qin unified China after conquering the six rival states, and the Warring States period came to an end. Ying Zheng, the king, named himself Emperor Shi Huang — literally meaning the "first emperor". Under this "first emperor", a unified Chinese empire under a complete autocratic system of state administration replaced those dukedoms and states under the system of enfeoffment. The country was divided into different administrative regions administered by officials appointed by the central government. This system, which featured centralization of authority, had been practiced until China's last feudal dynasty, the Qing, was toppled in the 1911 Revolution and the

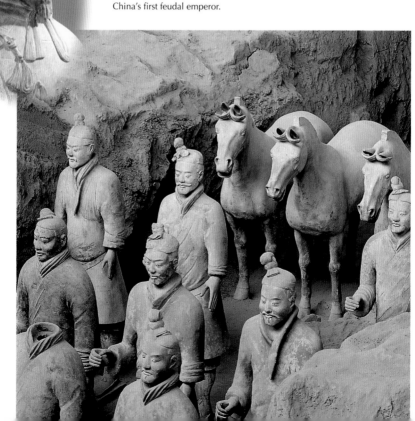

A terracotta general in the underground "army" meant to guard the tomb of Emperor Shi Huang of the Qin Dynasty, China's first feudal emperor.

Terracotta soldiers and battle steeds in the underground army.

country became a public. The written language and the weights and measures, which used to be different from state to state, were unified under Emperor Shi Huang, who also ordered building of state roads according to unified standards. These measures were obviously conducive to economic and cultural development and communication between different regions. Nevertheless, the emperor, a downright dictator, was notorious for the damage he did on the Chinese culture. He ordered burning of all historic records in archives except those written by historians of the State of Qin. He also ordered that all books, except those of fortune telling, medicine and crop farming, were to be handed over to the government and burned. The golden age in the history of China's ideological development, an age of contention between different schools of thoughts that featured the entire East Zhou period, came to an abrupt end due to these incredible measures for control of people's thinking.

To ward off invasions of nomadic tribes living in the north, the states of Qin, Zhao and Yan had built wall fortifications along their northern borders. The "first emperor" had these linked and extended east and westward to form the 5,000 km-long Great Wall, which is now recognized as a world wonder. The emperor, who always craved for greatness and success, just couldn't bear to think what someday he was to die like everybody else. This prompted him to send out people to search for elixir of life on high seas while building a grandiose mausoleum for him so that even if he died, he would live in the same splendor and luxury as when he was alive. In recent decades, archeologists have unearthed a terracotta "army" supposedly to guard his mausoleum — 7,000 soldiers, 600 horses, more than 100 war chariots and numerous pieces of weaponry. The soldiers are about two meters tall, and are different from one another in facial expression and posture — all superb art works that are imposing in outlook with attention paid to every minute detail. Nobody knows how great a treasure house of cultural relics the mausoleum may eventually prove to be, as only a small

Bronze steed with a bird under a hoof, which may serve as material evidence to the existence of the Silk Road. It was excavated from a Han Dynasty (206 BC-220 AD) tomb in Wuwei County, Gansu Province.

part of the area it occupies has been opened for archeological excavation.

Though short-lived, the Qin Dynasty left a deep, lasting imprint on dynasties that followed it. After the Qin collapsed, wars were fought for a few years between rival peasant armies and the winner, Liu Bang, established the Han Dynasty. Historians divide the history of the new dynasty into two periods - West Han from 206 BC to 8 AD and East Han from 25 AD to 220 AD. The two periods were, however, disconnected because a high minister named Wang Mang usurped the throne and changed the title of the reigning dynasty into Xin, and ruled China from the eighth year to the 25th of the first century.

The Han dynasty practiced a policy of encouraging agricultural production while restricting commerce in its development. To show the public the importance they attached to agricultural production, the first few emperors of the dynasty customarily went to work in

Relieves on a brick in Han Dynasty (206 BC-220 AD) tomb depicts people harvesting crops.

the fields during a certain period of the year, and their wives followed suit by raising silkworms or planting mulberry trees in the palace complex. In contrast, merchants were forbidden to wear silk clothes and were forced to pay heavy taxes, and neither they nor their children were allowed to hold official posts. Practices like these, in fact, adversely affected China's social and economic development.

In the Han Dynasty, the Chinese invented papermaking and developed a firing process to produce porcelain ware. In the first century under the Han Dynasty, the country had a population of 59.5 million. Relieves on bricks excavated from Han tombs bring to life many aspects of life under the reign of the dynasty. The family was the basic unit of agricultural production. In a given family, women had the task of raising silkworms. In north China, weaving was a family handicraft industry, but there were also fairly large textile mills run by the government. Rich families enjoyed themselves over song and dance performances at private parties, which also featured performances of acrobatics and magic shows.

Despite its growing might, the dynasty faced threats from the neighboring Xiongnu (the Huns) in the north. These nomads not only frequently invaded and harassed areas south of the Gobi but also enslaved small states in the West Region encompassing what is now Xinjiang Uyghur Autonomous Region of China and some of the Central Asian republics. Emperor Wu Di of the Han Dynasty, a statesman of great talent and broad vision who reigned supreme from 140 BC to 87 BC, repeatedly sent expedition forces against the Xiongnu tribes, forcing them either to surrender or move to farther north. Beginning as of 138 BC, the emperor twice sent Zhang Qian as the imperial envoy to the West Region for communication with states there. Zhang Qian and those after him sent China's techniques of iron smelting and methods for building irrigation facilities to the West Region and, in the course of the exchange, fruit and musical instruments of the West Region were introduced to China. The opening of land routes ushered in a boom in trade between China and states to its west. Of the Chinese commodities introduced to these states, silk and silk cloth were the best received, hence the term "Silk Road" in reference to those ancient trade routes. As the civilization of the Han Dynasty became increasingly influential outside the country, the Chinese came to be referred to as "*han ren*" or the "Han people" in Asian countries and countries even farther away. And as time went by, "Hanzu" (the Han ethnic group) replaced "Huaxia zu" (the ethnic group of Huaxia[3]) as the official name for China's ethnic majority group.

Han Dynasty rulers designated Confucianism as the orthodox

Hunting as depicted on a mural of the West Wei Dynasty (535-556). The mural is seen in one of the Mogao grottoes, Gansu Province.

or state ideology and, on their order, schools of the central and local levels were set up. In another development, the dynasty initiated the system of selecting government officials through imperial examination. In the first century AD, Buddhism spread to the east via those trade routes and, with imperial support, it soon became popular in China. Meanwhile, there emerged Taoism, the indigenous religion. Sima Qian (145 BC-90 BC), an imperial historian, authored the *Records of the Historian*. This is the first book of general history ever produced in China. It describes legends from the time of the mythical Huangdi (Yellow Emperor) and events that had happened from the Shang and Zhou periods to Sima Qian's own times - a span of 3,000 years.

China came to be divided amid chaos for a long time after the Han Dynasty collapsed. It was divided into the Kingdom of Wei (220-265) in the north, the Shu (221-263) in the Sichuan Basin on the upper reaches of the Yangtze River and the Wu (222-280) in areas on the middle and lower reaches of the Yangtze River. After a tripartite confrontation that went on for decades, the Wei defeated the Shu. But shortly afterwards, a powerful minister named Sima toppled the Wei and made himself emperor of the Jin - or the West Jin as historians call it. In the year 280, the Jin conquered the Wu, and China was again a united country.

But before long, eight princes of the West Jin began fighting one another and the tangled warfare lasted for as long as 16 years. Greatly weakened, the West Jin came extinct in 316. Then came the East Jin in 317, with the emperor picked up by those aristocrats and ranking officials of the West Jin who fled to the south. The East Jin ruled south China for more than 100 years before it died out in 420. From the time of the East Jin's collapse to China's reunification in 589, four dynasties -Song, Qi, Liang and Chen - ruled south China in succession. The Southern Dynasties, so to speak, all had their capital in what is now Nanjing.

From 304 to 439, five ethnic groups set up a string of regimes in areas north of the Yangtze River, and so did the Han Chinese in

Buddhist statues of the fifth century at Longmen Grottoes, Luoyang City, Henan Province. Grotto art thrived in the fifth and sixth centuries along with the spread of Buddhism in China.

southwest China. The so-called "period of the 16 states" ended in 439 when the North Wei reunified north China. But not long afterwards, the North Wei split into two parts, which were to be replaced by new regimes. From 439 to 581, five regimes - or the "Five Dynasties" - reigned supreme in north China. Political regimes that came in succession in both the north and the south are referred to as the "North-South Dynasties". The country's split lasted for more than 160 years, from 420 to 589. During this period, seesaw battles were fought between those in the north and those in the south, with victories and defeats hanging in the balance.

From the third to the sixth century, south China was relatively peaceful, and this prompted a mass migration from the north to the south - in fact the first large-scale population flow in the Chinese history. The south benefited not only from increased labor power as a result of this population flow, but also from advanced production techniques brought in by immigrants from the north. While the south was enjoying an economic boom, the north witnessed merger of the various ethnic groups at an accelerating speed. Ever since the East Han period, increasing numbers of nomads in China's northwest moved eastward and came to live with the Han majority. While shifting to farming or semi-farming, they were keen to adopt ways of the Hans in organizing the state structure, formulating laws, setting up schools and promoting Confucianism, and intermarriages between Hans and people of ethnic minority groups became common. Meanwhile, cultures and folkways of ethnic minority groups were able to influence the Hans. Thanks to this merger, marked changes took place in languages, clothing and customs of all ethnic groups.

"Misfortune comes as a blessing to poets" - this old saying seems to fit in so well with the development of literature and art when China split, in succession, into the Three Kingdoms, the West Jin, the East Jin and the North-South Dynasties. Wars and internal conflicts failed to prevent the Chinese culture from developing. In fact, Chinese poetry and arts thrived amid wars and internal conflicts. Just one example: this chaotic historic period produced several masters of Chinese calligraphy credited with epoch-making accomplishments. The hard times compelled numerous scholars and aristocrats to withdraw from society and live in seclusion. And for the same reason, the entire society became religious when the vast majority of the Chinese people converted either to Buddhism or Taoism - in some cases to both. That explains why in the fifth century and on, people built so many grottoes. The Yungang Grottoes in Datong of Shanxi and Longmen Grottoes in Luoyang

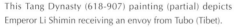

This Tang Dynasty (618-907) painting (partial) depicts Emperor Li Shimin receiving an envoy from Tubo (Tibet).

An orchestra on camel back, a masterpiece of the Tang Dynasty (618-907) tricolor glazed pottery. Tricolor glazed pottery objects were normally used as burial objects.

of Henan built during this period are, as a matter of fact, are treasure houses of Buddhist and Taoist art. In some aspects the Sui Dynasty (581-618) was similar to the Qin. The Sui reunified China in 589 and, immediately afterwards, took measures to strengthen control by the central government over local administration. Six ministries were set up under the central government, separately in charge of personnel, education, judicial, defense and other state affairs. The dynasty also institutionalized the imperial examination system for selection of government officials to replace the system of the preceding dynasties under which the fate of a candidate for officialdom was often determined by local government recommendation or family status. The succeeding dynasties inherited at least two things from the Sui - the central government structure and the imperial examination system. The Sui also had to its credit the digging of the Grand Canal, a 1,000-km man-made waterway from Hangzhou in the south to Beijing in the north, and sections of the canal are still open to navigation today.

Like the Qin, the Sui was short-lived even though it enjoyed prosperity in its first few years. The Sui was succeeded by the Tang (618-907), under which feudal China enjoyed an unprecedented economic prosperity and political might.

Sound economic policies and wise political strategies that the succeeding Tang Dynasty pursued in its early period prepared China for economic prosperity and imbued it with a confidence in embracing alien cultures. In fact none of the other dynasties in feudal China were as open as the Tang. More than 70 countries traded goods or had cultural exchanges with China via the Silk Road. The government encouraged foreign merchants to come for business and forbade officials to levy heavy taxes on them. Meanwhile, foreigners were allowed to settle in China, marry Chinese and even took official posts. What are now Guangzhou in Guangdong and Quanzhou in Fujian served as international trading ports. The national capital, Chang'an (what is now Xi'an in Shaanxi), was a thriving international metropolis with a population of more than 1 million including bevies of diplomatic emissaries, merchants and students from Persia (Iran), the Arab World, states on the Indian Peninsula, Japan and the Roman Empire. Through these foreigners, China's papermaking, textile and porcelain production techniques were introduced to the Arab world, and from the Arab World, spread further west to Africa and Europe. The Japanese were especially keen to learn from the Chinese culture. They took China as the model in everything, ranging from political system to architectural style, from the way women were dressed to the game of encirclement called *wei qi* in Chinese or *go* in Japanese. For so high an international prestige China enjoyed under the Tang Dynasty, the Chinese people came to be called *Tang ren* or the "Tang people" — a reference still being used to the Chinese in many countries of today.

The self-confidence and openness of the dynasty to alien cultures were also manifested in its handling of religious affairs. The government ensured complete freedom of religious belief. Under such a policy, indigenous and alien religions enjoyed equal status, each able to build up a group of believers. The Tang Dynasty was the golden age for Buddhism and Taoism. Meanwhile, Islam introduced from the Arab world and Nestorianism from the Mediterranean region each gained a place in China.

Science and culture enjoyed as great a boom as economy. The government attached a great importance to education, and large numbers of students and scholars from China's ethnic groups and surrounding countries came to study in Chang'an. Schools were beginning to offer specialized courses - medicine, mathematics, astronomy, etc. Printing with engraved wood blocks, which was started in the Sui Dynasty, was put to widespread use. The efficiency was thus multiplied for reproduction of Buddhist scripts and calendars, and collections of poetry by the best poets were printed for sale on the open market. To sum up, this combination of papermaking and printing came as a boost to cultural dissemination. In the late Tang period, gunpowder, which was originally used to produce sound and light effects in acrobatics and theatrical performances, came to be used for military purposes. Gunpowder was later introduced to the Arab world, along with knowledge of traditional Chinese medicine and the secret Taoist

Lady Gaoguo in Spring Outing, a masterpiece of the Tang Dynasty (618-907) painting.

art of making pills of immortality. In the 13th or the 14th century, gunpowder found its way from the Arab world to Europe.

The Tang Dynasty was the golden age for Chinese poetry, calligraphy and grotto art. The dynasty also produced some of the best painters in feudal China. Of those grottoes found in China, the Mogao Grottoes in Dunhuang, Gansu Province, are a treasure of cultural relics recognized the world over for their historic, cultural and artistic value. Tang Dynasty music and dancing commanded a unique demeanor mirroring the country's prosperity and might. With a vivid alien flavor, these testified to China's growing foreign contacts.

After the Tang Dynasty's doom, China again fell apart. From 907 to 960, five dynasties took control of zhong yuan or the Central Region. In chronicle division of the Chinese history, this was the "period of five dynasties". In south China, there emerged nine states, breaking into those that either existed simultaneously and those that ruled the same territories in succession. These nine, plus one in the north, comprised what historians call the "period of ten states".

In 960, the chaotic period of five dynasties and ten states ended

Festival of Pure Brightness on the River done by South Song Dynasty artist Zhang Zeduan. It depicts the bustling life of Bianliang, the national capital, now Kaifeng City of Henan Province.

A Song Dynasty (960-1279) porcelain pillow.

when the Song Dynasty, with Bianliang (what is now Kaifeng, Henan Province) as capital, was founded. The dynasty was bold enough to launch some political and economic reforms - unfortunately to no avail due to resistance from conservatives within the ruling class. Even worse was that from the very beginning, the Song Dynasty faced threats from a few tribes in the north. Purely nomadic in the past, these tribes had, by shifting to agriculture and learning from the Hans their advanced production techniques, grown powerful enough to challenge the supremacy of the Song Dynasty. Large-scale invasions by these tribes eventually forced the Song government to move in 1127 to areas south of the Yangtze River and designated what is now Hangzhou, Zhejiang Province, as its capital. Historians refer the Song Dynasty before 1127 as the North Song, and after 1127, as the South Song.

Despite its weakness in wars and diplomacy, the Song Dynasty achieved the most significant economic progress so far in the history of feudal China. From the 10th to the 13th century, areas south of the Yangtze River were relatively peaceful, prompting one more massive migration from the north to the south. The south eventually outstripped the north in agricultural production, a process accompanied by a rapid development of sea and river transport while the population kept growing. It was under the Song Dynasty that China's economic gravity began shifting to the south.

As industry and commerce flourished, numerous urban towns sprang up round cities and near hubs of communication in the countryside, some serving as commodity distribution centers while others, as centers of printing or porcelain production. A new way of urban life came into being. In cities and urban towns, shops selling daily necessities and other goods were within easy reach of residents. So were those *wa si* - recreation centers operating for a profit - that offered rich repertoires of theatrical, acrobatic and martial art performances as well as story telling.

In the early 11th century, 16 rich merchants in Sichuan Province jointly issued *jiao zi* - the earliest paper currency in the world. In both the North Song and South Song periods, China's domestic and foreign trade flourished. According to historic records, by the mid-12th century, incomes from foreign trade had already come to account as much as 15% of the state revenue. Chinese vessels were calling ports in Southeast Asia, on the coast of the Indian Ocean and the Arabian Peninsula and on the east coast of Africa. China led the world in shipbuilding and sea navigation. Ocean-going vessels of the Song Dynasty sailed directly to destinations in two dozen countries and regions. The country was, for the first time, able to directly trade goods in massive quantities with foreign countries, without having to rely on foreign middlemen as in the past.

Also during the Song Dynasty typeset printing, compasses for sea navigation, textile mills propelled by water force and leakage-proof vessel boards were developed. These inventions represented the highest achievements in scientific and technological development ever made in China, from which other countries on the Eurasian Continent were to benefit as well. British philosopher Francis Bacon (1561-1626) spoke highly of printing, gunpowder and navigation compasses, noting that these inventions changed the outlook and conditions of the entire world. He said that no empire, religious sect or individual could have exerted so strong an influence on human development as these inventions made by the Chinese.

Cultural achievements of the Song Dynasty were also remarkable. Confucianism became even more closely associated with the country's political philosophy and able to exert a still stronger ideological influence through fusion with Buddhist and Taoist doctrines. The imperial examination system improved, in such a way as to allow still more intellectuals to compete for official posts. Private schools flourished, and many of them have had their sites preserved to this day. The dynasty represented one more golden age for ci^4 poetry, painting and calligraphy since the Tang Dynasty.

The Yuan Dynasty (1279-1368) succeeded the Song. That dyansty was, in fact, the first political regime set up by

Men Tending Crops and Women Weaving, a Yuan Dynasty (1271-1368) painting of country life.

an ethnic minority group that reigned supreme over the entire China. In the early 13th century, Genghis Khan conquered the various Mongol tribes and then started massive expansionist wars. Mongol armies under the command of his descendents swept across the Eurasian Continent, reaching the Danube Valley while driving southward. They did succeeded in establishing a huge Eurasian empire, but before long, the empire fell apart into several independent states. In the Central Region of China, the Mongols set up a new dynasty called Yuan. Dadu (the "grand capital"), or what is now Beijing, was made the national capital, which was to remain as such for the following two dynasties, the Ming and the Qing.

From the Five Dynasties period to the Yuan Dynasty, the various ethnic groups of the Chinese nation experienced further cultural assimilation. Back in the Tang Dynasty, many Persians and Arabs who believed in Islam came to settle in China. Beginning as of the end of the 13th century, China once again received large numbers of Persian and Arab immigrants who, living together with people of the Hans, Mongols and people of other ethnic groups, eventually formed a new ethnic group called Hui.

New developments were made in the Yuan Dynasty in textile and porcelain production. Cotton cloth became the main material for clothing of people living in areas south of the Yangtze River, and silk cloth and porcelain ware were China's major export commodities. The Dynasty maintained trade relations with many countries in Asia, Africa and Europe. Quanzhou in Fujian was the country's largest trading port, which was good enough to accommodate hundreds of ocean-going vessels at a time. Residential areas special for Persians and Arabs, along with mosques, were built in the city. The Yuan Dynasty China played host to many people from overseas — mostly merchants, and not a few foreigners residing in China held official posts in the government. The best-known guest coming from afar was Marco Polo, an Italian traveler, who visited many places during his stay

Theatrical performance as depicted on a Yuan Dynasty (1271-1368) mural.

in the country. Marco Polo's travel notes, which among other things provide vivid descriptions of prosperity in cities like Dadu and Hangzhou, prompted many Europeans to look forward to going to China and seeing it for themselves.

The dynasty represented an important period in the development of Chinese literature and art, and the achievements in theatrical creation were especially spectacular. Dadu, the country's political center, was the national "theatrical capital" as well, where large numbers of playwrights, poets and painters gathered. Guan Hanqing (?-1279), who was more than 300 years earlier than William Shakespeare, wrote more than 60 plays throughout his life and, for the artistic value and influence of his works, the playwright won a worldwide fame as the "Shakespeare of the Orient". Scholars of the Yuan Dynasty took a special liking of painting and calligraphy. Painters often expressed their feelings or emotions by drawing scenery, birds and flowers, from which the "scholarly painting" school originated and became the mainstream of the Chinese fine art.

Peasant rebellions drove the Mongols to where they had come from, to areas north of the Gobi. The Ming Dynasty (1368-1644) succeeded the Yuan. The new dynasty was the only political regime established by peasants who started rebellions in the south and fought all the way to the north until complete victory. China experienced an economic boom in the early Ming period. In 1405, Emperor Yong Le ordered Zheng He (1371-1435) to command a fleet of ocean-going vessels on a voyage to the "Western Ocean" — the parts of Southeast Asia to the west of Brunei and areas along the coast of the Indian Ocean. By 1433, Zhen He had completed seven voyages to more than 30 countries, reaching as far as the east coast of Africa and the Red Sea. The imperial fleet under his command comprised more than 200 vessels with 27,000 people on board including the crew, doctors, handicraftsmen and guards. Every time the fleet departed, it was loaded with silk cloth and porcelain ware, and returned with pearls and jewels, perfume, spices and medicinal materials. The distances covered by the voyages and the superb techniques used to build the vessels were a testament to China's status as the world's leading maritime power. But, after Emperor Yong Le died, the dynasty made a round about turn and banned maritime trade. The dramatic change in policy closed the country to international intercourse, and subsequently the national economy to international competition.

In the 16th century, sweet potato, maize, peanut, tobacco and other alien crops were introduced to China, which were soon to be sown to large areas. Porcelain production techniques improved even further, and Jingdezhen in Jiangxi Province rapidly expanded its production to become the country's "porcelain capital". The mid-Ming period witnessed the birth of textile workshops operating under the principle of "the owner furnishing the capital while the workers contributing labor", indicating that use of hired labor in industrial production began. Nevertheless, the country's industry and commerce continued to be handicapped in development under the same old policy of "encouraging farming while restricting commerce". Heavy taxes were imposed on industry and commerce, and that was only one of the numerous government measures to minimize their growth. The government and local despots monopolized the production and distribution of numerous commodities. Unlike their counterparts in the West, Chinese merchants had a low social status and were denied of access to political power. In short, effort to develop a market-oriented economy in China was hampered from the very beginning.

China had been ahead of the world in scientific development until the 15th century, but further development was difficult for lack of a motive force. The Ming Dynasty was credited with fairly good achievements in development of water conservation and medicine, and publication of *Guide to Farming (Nongzhen Quanshu)*, *Exploitation of the Works of Nature (Tiangong Kaiwu)*, *Compendium of Materia (Bencao Gangmu)* and other encyclopaedias in different branches of science. Short stories and novels became the mainstream of the Ming Dynasty literature. Theatrical creation and performances continued to flourish and, in many parts of south China, watching performances of local operas was the main cultural activity of the public.

As their predecessors, scholars of the Ming Dynasty liked painting and calligraphy and were good at them.

Porcelain jar of the Ming Dynasty (1368-1644).

A well-preserved section of the Great Wall built in the Ming Dynasty (1368-1644).

Ming Dynasty structures can still be seen nowadays, ranging from sections of the Great Wall that underwent major repairs under the Ming government to the Forbidden City built under Emperor Yong Le, and from walled courtyards for ordinary people in Beijing to private gardens for aristocrats and rich merchants in Suzhou. These structures are material evidence to the feudal ethnical code that called for explicit distinction between the ruler and the ruled and between the high and the low. Not to mention the layout of structures in the Forbidden City and the colors and designs of their walls and roofs. Even in a walled courtyard in Beijing, differences between the "principal" and "side" rooms are clearly discernible[5].

The Qing Dynasty (1644-1911), which was set up by the Manchu ethnic group, was China's last feudal dynasty. The country enjoyed relative peace and stability during the first 100 years of the dynasty. And during that period, China had an edge in international trade, and Chinese tea, porcelain ware, raw silk and silk cloth sold well in Europe, Japan and Russia. Industry and commerce were better developed than in the preceding dynasty — in fact attained the highest level of development for the entire history of feudal China

Road leading to the 13 Imperial tombs of the Ming Dynasty (1368-1644) in Changping County under the jurisdiction of Beijing Municipality. Note the stone statues of generals and officials on either side of the road, which served as the imperial guard of honor for the emperor in the nether world.

A collective portrait of the 13 performing artists of Peking Opera who were recognized as the best in China under Emperor Tong Zhi (1862-1874) and the succeeding emperor, Guang Xu (1875-1908). Note the artists' facial make-ups and stage costumes.

in terms of the scale of production, division of labor and technological sophistication. Nevertheless, small-scale farming combined with family handicraft production continued to dominate the Chinese society and economy. As ever, families produced for self-sufficiency, not for the market.

As under the Ming, creation of novels and theatrical works flourished under the Qing, and so did architectural engineering. Many of the things people are still enjoying — the landmark classical Chinese novel *Dreams of the Red Chamber,* Peking Operas, the Summer Palace in Beijing, to name just a few — are cultural achievements made in the Qing period. A few scholars of the early Qing period had vague ideas of democratic enlightenment and called for it. But their voices were subdued under the high-handed imperial policy of ideological control, and classics of Confucianism continued to be worshipped as the orthodox political and cultural philosophy. European missionaries brought to China advanced scientific knowledge, including mathematics, astronomy, calendar and physics, and Emperor Kang Xi, who ruled the country from 1662 to 1723, was keen to study them. But never did the dynasty work in real earnest to promote science development. Their thinking shackled by the imperial examination system, Chinese intellectuals customarily took light of learning things of practical use. At the turn of the 18th century, the Industrial Revolution had by and large been completed in Europe, which came as a boost to

Interior of the Hall of Heavenly Purity in the Forbidden City, Beijing. The hall was where emperors of the Ming and Qing dynasties handled court affairs. Note the imperial throne or "dragon chair" in the middle.

the development of human civilization. In contrast, the Qing government continued to close the country to economic and cultural intercourse with other countries. Once ahead of the world, it was falling farther and farther behind the West, and becoming increasingly vulnerable to foreign aggression. In 1840, Britain launched the Opium War against China. In 1865, the Anglo-French allied forces seized Beijing in the Second Opium War. Soldiers stormed into the Garden of Perfect Splendor[6], set it ablaze, and pillaged those cultural treasures there. In the last decades of the 19th century, China fell prey to ever-intensifying attempts of Britain, France, Japan, Germany, Russia, the United States and other imperialist powers to carve it up.

The Qing Dynasty was toppled in the 1911 Revolution, and gone was the system of autocratic monarchy that had held sway for more than 2,000 years. The Chinese people fought over the following decades for an independent, democratic and powerful China. In 1949, at the end of the wars for national independence and people's liberation, the People's Republic of China was born, and a new page was opened in the country's history.

1. The culture is named after Yangshao Village, Mianchi County, Henan Province, where its was found for the first time.

2. Round pieces of jade with a hole in the middle (used for ceremonial purposes in ancient China).

3. "Huaxia" is the archaic name for Zhongguo or China.

4. *Ci* poems, which originated in the Tang Dynasty, are written to certain tunes with strict tonal patterns and rhyme schemes, and in fixed numbers of lines and words.

5. The "principal" room in a typical courtyard in Beijing normally faces south, which is flanked by "side" rooms that face east or west. In old times, the principal room was always reserved for the eldest male member of the family and his wife who had absolute power in the management of family affairs.

6. The Garden of Perfect Splendor on the western outskirts of Beijing was the world's largest and most beautiful imperial garden in the world of the 18th and 19th centuries.

The Square-Shape Characters

Vitality of Chinese Characters

Hanyu or Chinese is China's official language. Modern Chinese is spoken not only by people of the Han ethnic group, but is also used by all ethnic groups of the Chinese nation as the common vehicle of communication. Besides, it is one of the six working languages of the United Nations. Chinese characters are signs to record oral Chinese with. In shape, they look like "squares" that are independent of one another.

People using a written language of an alphabetic system can spell a word out on hearing it spoken or pronounce it when seeing it, provided they know the pronunciation of the alphabets and the spelling rules. The Chinese characters, however, are not that simple. Characters vastly different in meaning are often pronounced the same way, and the same character may have vastly different meanings or be pronounced in different ways. It is indeed difficult for learners to recognize Chinese characters and learn them by heart at the beginning.

When we examine the structure of the Chinese characters, we find that they are formed with strokes in a variety of shapes. Strokes in Chinese characters assume more than two dozen shapes that fall into five basic categories: *dian* (dot stroke), *heng* (horizontal stroke), *shu* (vertical stroke), *pie* (curved stroke) and *zhe* (angular stroke). The number of strokes that form a single Chinese character ranges from a few to more than a dozen. Because of this, many people think that Chinese characters are too complicated in structure to write – relative to alphabetic languages, of course. It is difficult to learn the Chinese language also because of the sheer number of its characters. Characters still in use are counted at somewhere between 6,000 and 7,000, including about 3,000 that are most frequently used.

Despite that, the Chinese language has always had a great vitality.

Jia gu wen, or inscriptions on bones or tortoise shells that date to the Shang period (16th-11th century BC) are the earliest Chinese characters in a complete system. These inscriptions are already quite sophisticated in structure and meaning. This prompts the assumption that before coming into being, Chinese characters must have undergone a long period of evolution. Of the most important ideographs that once existed, the cuneiform characters of ancient Babylonia and Assyria and the pictographs of ancient Egypt came to extinction a long, long time ago. In contrast, the Chinese characters have come down in one continuous line. Moreover, in many ways the Chinese characters we are using resemble those used thousands of years ago.

The Chinese characters are a refraction of the Chinese culture that dates to several thousand years ago, and analysis of their structure and earliest form to trace them to their root brings to light the mentality, customs and habits of the ancient Chinese. Take, for example the character, 取 (pronounced as *qu*, meaning "fetch"). The left part of the character, 耳, is the pictograph of the ear, and the right part, 又, the hand. In ancient wars a victorious warrior often cut off the ears of a dead enemy as evidence when reporting the victory to his commander.

Handwritten text left over from the Tang Dynasty.

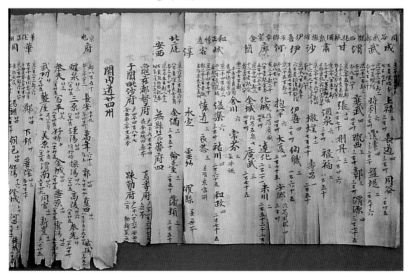

Examples like this are numerous, and that justifies the scholarly assertion that by "deciphering" the Chinese characters, one is in fact learning the Chinese history.

The expressiveness of the Chinese characters transcends both time and space. As time goes by, the pronunciation of many characters has changed, but no change has taken place in their basic structure and meaning. Because of this, people of today can still read books and records in their original that date to 2,000 or even 3,000 years ago. Dialects are vastly different from place to place in China, but that does not affect the basic meaning of the characters. As a matter of fact, this common written language has been vital to the unity of the Chinese nation and to the continuity of the Chinese history.

German philosopher and mathematician G. W. Leibuniz of the 17th century once envisaged a common written language for people of all nationalities, a written language not to be affected by changes in time and space. The written Chinese, in fact, is a language that fits in with his expectations.

Evolution of the Chinese Characters in Forms

As time goes by, however, there have been changes in ways Chinese characters are written. Inscriptions on bones and tortoise shells are Chinese characters in their earliest known form, and inscriptions on ancient bronze objects came next. Along with the development of the Chinese society, Chinese characters became increasingly diverse in form, culminating in the four basic forms or styles: *zhuan* (seal characters), *kai shu* (regular script), *cao shu* (cursive script) and *xing shu* (running hand).

Inscriptions on bones and tortoise shells or *jia gu wen* date to the Shang period (16th century BC-11th century BC), when superstition prevailed. Before doing anything important, people would undergo a ritual to have the outcome foretold – what would become of the harvest for the year, whether a war could be won or whether a hunting expedition would fetch anything, etc. They would drill a hole in a piece of animal bone or tortoise shell, bake the piece on light fire, and

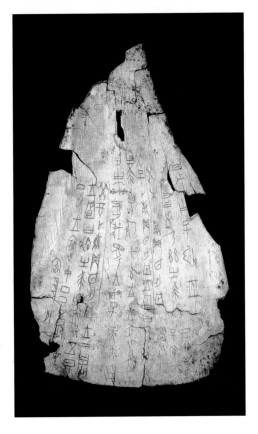

A piece of oracle bone dating to more than 3,000 years ago. The inscriptions, which are Chinese characters of the earliest known form, tell about the chariot used by a Shang sovereign and one of his hunting expeditions.

decide whether to go ahead by judging the shape and direction of the cracks. Then a historian would cut the judgement on the piece. Oracle bones were first discovered in 1899 and, since then, about 150,000 pieces have been found. Inscriptions on them comprise some 4,600 individual characters, of which 1,700 have had their meaning identified. Though pictographs, these inscriptions are highly sophisticated as components of a written language.

Inscriptions on ancient bronze objects are known to experts as *jin wen* – literally meaning "metal inscriptions". As tripods (*ding*) were the most important ritual vessels of the Shang period and bells (*zhong*) the most important musical instrument, *jin wen* or "metal inscriptions" are also known as *zong ding wen* or "bell-tripod inscriptions". Inscriptions on a bronze artifact tell who was its owner, for what reason or purpose the artifact was produced, etc. In structure, *Jin wen* or *zong ding wen* inscriptions are basically the same as *jia gu wen* or inscriptions on oracle bones, except for differences in the shape of some strokes.

During the Spring and Autumn and Warring States periods (770 BC -221 BC), Chinese characters were in a variety of forms, each for use just in one of the numerous dukedoms or states that ruled different parts of the Yangtze and Yellow River basins. This state of affairs obviously hampered use of Chinese as the common language. Emperor Shi Huang of the Qin Dynasty, who unified the entire country, ordered adoption of *xiao zhuan* or "the lesser seal character" as the official form of Chinese characters. *Xiao zhuan* scripts are rectangular in form and are neat in structure.

What the emperor did was in fact the first nationwide campaign in China's history to standardize the Chinese scripts, and it established the basic square shape of Chinese characters. *Jia gu wen, jin wen and xiao zhuan,* which are broadly referred to as "ancient Chinese scripts", are no longer in practical use. In traditional art forms like calligraphy and seal cutting, however, they are still important as artistic styles.

Xiao zhuan scripts were used mainly in government records. But ordinary people still found it difficult to write, hence their evolution into *da zhuan* or "greater seal character". *Da zhuan* scripts are easier to write, as many "arch" or cursive strokes characteristic of *xiao zhuan* scripts are straightened to varying degrees to form straight or angular strokes. Creation of *Da zhuan* scripts suggests that the China's written language lost its pictographic character, which in turn means that it was to become increasingly easy for use.

Kai shu, the standard style of Chinese characters, was a development of *li shu* scripts. It came to be popular in the late Han Dynasty and has been in use since then as the most popular style of Chinese characters. In addition to standard forms such as *xiao zhuan* and *kai shu,* Chinese characters are written in two supplementary forms, namely, *cao shu* and *xing shu. Cao shu* scripts are *li shu* scripts that can be written at a fast speed with the characters in a broad, free outline. For this reason, characters in *cao shu* style are somewhat difficult to read. *Xing shu* scripts are something in between scripts in *li shu* and *cao shu* styles. Easy to write and read, *xing shu* is suitable for practical use like *li shu*.

The same Chinese character may be in two forms, namely, the complex form and simplified form. A character in the complex form normally has many strokes, while the same character in the simplified form has fewer strokes. Assumption by the same character of both forms has been common since ancient times, hence the need for the government to promote use of characters in the simplified form to standardize written Chinese and facilitate its use. To meet the urgent need to promote education and eradicate illiteracy among people, the Chinese Government has since 1949 done a tremendous amount of work to standardize the written language and push for use of simplified characters. Several batches of simplified characters have been decreed for use in the country. Use of characters in standard simplified form has not only promoted the literacy campaign but also made it possible for students to spend less time on learning in order to become able to read and write. In Hong Kong, Macao and Taiwan, however, characters in the complex form are still used due

A bronze kettle left over from the Warring States Period (475 BC-221 BC).

A list of 12 inscriptions on animal bones or tortoise shells and the corresponding characters used today.

The character 明 (pronounced "ming", meaning "bright") written in different calligraphic styles (from top to bottom): *xiao zhuan* (seal character), *li shu* (official script), *kai shu* (regular script), *xing shu* (running hand) and *cao shu* (cursive script).

The present form of the character 取 (right, pronounced as "qu", meaning "fetch") and the corresponding inscriptions on ancient bronze objects (middle) and on animal bones or tortoise shells (left).

to historic reasons.

Ways of Composing Chinese Characters

According to historic records, far back in the Warring States period, the Chinese, through analysis of the basic structures of characters then in use, already established the *liu shu* theory – meaning division of Chinese characters into six basic categories according to their structures. But until the East Han Dynasty, nobody had been able to specify what the six categories exactly were. Xu Shen, an East Han Dynasty scholar, was the most prominent in cracking the mystery. In his *Explanations and Study of the Composition of Characters* (*Shuowen Jiezi*), he divided Chinese characters into the categories of *zhi yi*, *xiang xing*, *xing sheng*, *hui yi* and *jia jie*. Xu Shen's theory has been valued to this day, but it is generally recognized that *hui yi* (associative compounds) and *jia jie* (phonetic loan characters) are ways of using characters, not ways of composing them.

Xiang xing characters are pictographs, which are composed by "drawing" real things. Just a few examples: 日 (the sun), 口 (the mouth), 山 (mountain), and 羊 (sheep). It's easy to "draw" a thing with a simple physical outlook. But pictographs won't do when the meaning of something complicated or abstract has to be denoted.

A *zhi yi* character is a pictograph with a symbolic or indicative sign. Let's see the characters 上 (above, up or higher) and 下 (below, down or lower). Note the horizontal stroke, which is the "base line" for what is above and what is below. Another example is 本 meaning "fundamental", "root", etc. The basic part of the character is 木, which means "tree", and the horizontal stroke – the indicative stroke – shows where the root of the tree is. *Zhi yi* characters are even fewer in numbers than *xiang xing* pictographs because it is difficult to bring out the meaning of everything just with symbolic or indicative signs.

Hui yi means combining two or more characters into one to form a new character with a compound meaning. One example is 休, which means "have a rest". The characters consists of two parts, 人 (person) in its vertical form and 木 (tree) – when a person leans against a tree, well, he is having a rest. Let's see one more example, 信. The character also has two parts, 人 (person) in its vertical form and 言 (words). The compound character suggests that a person is trustworthy if he honors his words, hence its meaning "honesty".

A *Xing sheng* or picto-phonetic character also has two parts, the pictographic part and phonetic part. Let's examine two characters of this category, 枝 (meaning "tree branches") and 村 (meaning "village"). The character 木 (tree) is the pictographic part of either character because branches are parts of a tree and a village won't be called a village without trees. Meanwhile, 支 (pronounced "zhi") and 寸 (pronounced "cun") are the phonetic signs for the two characters. In other words, 枝 is pronounced the same way as 支, and 村 and 寸 have the same vowel. Put two characters – one denoting the shape of a thing and the other, the pronunciation – together and you create a new character, and that may explain why more than 80% of the characters currently in use are picto-phonetic. But things are not that simple. Due to a variety of factors including changes that have taken place since ancient times in pronouncing the same characters, about three fourths of the picto-phonetic characters are not pronounced the same way as their phonetic parts. Because of this, people can be easily confused.

As time goes by, the same characters may have had their forms or meaning changed. But the Chinese characters have remained under a complete system of ideography, and their forms, closely associated with what they mean. By using the *liu shu* theory to analyze the composition of a character, one may understand what it was intended to mean when it was concocted, and therefore find it easier to read works in classical Chinese.

Calligraphy – a Traditional Art Form

As linguistic signs and a tool for communication, Chinese characters are certainly meant for practical use. But ways of writing characters have eventually developed into an art form – calligraphy or *shu fa* as the Chinese call it.

Two factors have made this development possible. One is the pictographic nature of Chinese characters in their earliest form, and the other, use of writing brushes. A writing brush has a bamboo or wooden shaft and a tip of animal hair. The tip of a writing brush is

Calligraphic works cut on a cliff on Mt. Taishan, one of China's best known scenic places. Since about 2,000 years ago, men of letters have often had their hand-written words cut on Mt. Taishan cliffs.

often made of hair of different animals, so that it will be soft while elastic – good enough for writing with. The calligrapher dips the tip in ink and, wielding the shaft with different hand movements, produces characters on the paper – not characters in their conventional sense, but something of artistic or appreciative value. To be a real calligrapher, one needs to learn a host of skills for wielding the writing brush – in fact one has to undergo rigorous training to master these skills. Writing brushes are often seen as a symbol of the spirit unique of the Chinese as a people. It is much more difficult to write or paint with a writing brush than with a pen, especially when anatomical precision is required. But persons with a good command of the skills can be in their element when writing or drawing, and can thus produce beautiful things.

Chinese calligraphy, as an art form, experienced its first heyday during the Wei-Jin period from the third to the fourth century, when scripts in all styles – *zhuan shu, li shu, kai shu, cao shu* and *xing shu* – came into being and developed into different schools of calligraphic art. Wang Xizhi (307-365), the "sage of Chinese calligraphy", was the most prominent of all calligraphers and, among his works, those in

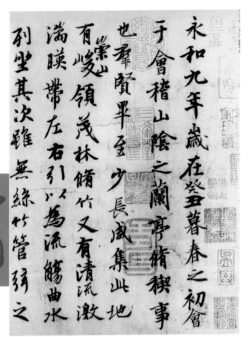

Preface to the Orchid Pavilion Collection in the handwriting of Wang Xizhi (307-365), the "sage of Chinese calligraphy".

the *xing shu* or running hand style are recognized as the best. In the Tang Dynasty, China enjoyed unprecedented prosperity and, as a result, calligraphy again flourished. In schools, calligraphy was a compulsory course. The dynasty produced a string of master calligraphers representing the highest achievements in all styles. Calligraphy in *kai shu* or the regular script style, in particular, reached so high an artistic level that even today's calligraphers find it difficult to scale. Yan Zhenqing (709-785) and Liu Gongquan (778-865) were the greatest calligraphic maters of the Tang period. Their works have been modeled after until today. In learning to write with a brush, one has had to trace over reproductions of characters written by master calligraphers.

Chinese calligraphy and traditional Chinese painting are both arts of lines – "of the same origin" as the saying goes. In fact painters often use calligraphic skills in drawing. There is another saying to the effect that both calligraphy and painting are associated with dancing, in that lines forming calligraphic works and paintings are as imaginative and graceful as dancing movements. Here is a story that has been passed down from the Tang Dynasty: Zhang Xu, a calligrapher, developed a unique *cao shu* or cursive script style by drawing inspiration from sword dancing. There is no way to have the truth of the story confirmed, but it is a fact that rhythm, movement and proper arrangement of characters and lines are as vital to calligraphy as to dancing.

In ancient China, most calligraphers were scholars or officials with an intellectual background, and many were well versed in poetry, painting, music, dancing, history, philosophy, etc. Ever since ancient times, the way characters are written has been taken as a revelation of the inner world of the calligrapher, his self-cultivation, emotions and way of life, hence this old saying: the characters mirror the image of the calligrapher, and the style is the man. A similar saying goes something like this: calligraphy grows out of the "heart" (the inner world) of the calligrapher.

More often than not, Chinese children start learning calligraphy the day they start learning the characters. As a practice, they would keep copying models by master calligraphers day after day – maybe for more than ten years in a row. Only the most gifted, most hardworking few would eventually be recognized as calligraphers, but people in their tens of millions would keep practicing all their lives. As the Chinese see it, doing calligraphy is a way of self-cultivation, a way of tempering one's willpower.

Calligraphy can be put to practical use, as shown by inscriptions written in honor of people or events or on shop signs. Works by master calligraphers are seen as treasures, hung on walls of studies or kept in private collections of which only the most intimate friends or the most honored guests could have a glimpse.

Dongba pictographs used by the Naxis,
one of China's minority groups.

A Family of Languages

Chinese is not the only language spoken in China. The country boasts a variety of languages spoken by people of the various ethnic minority groups. Like the official language, these mirror the cultural development of their speakers and have undergone changes over the milleniums.

Some ethnic minority groups are still using pictographs. The Naxis, for example, are using a pictographic system called *"Dongba"* that came into being eight or nine centuries ago. There are also ethnic groups using syllabic languages. People of the Yi ethic group, for example, use a written language developed on the basis of *Cuan*, a syllabic language created by their ancestors. But more ethnic minority groups prefer alphabetic systems. Some of the alphabetic languages are dead, and those still alive include the Tibetan, Mongolian and Dai languages.

Chinese influenced the languages of minority ethnic groups in their development. In ancient China, some minority ethnic groups took Chinese as the model in creating their own written languages. The Xixia[1] scripts, one of the dead languages, have the same components of Chinese characters.

Tang Dynasty (618-907) books in paper rolls.

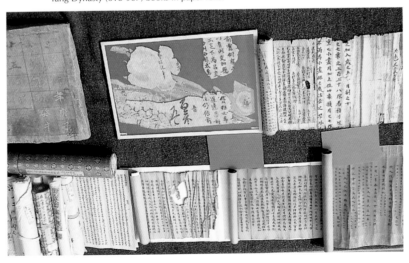

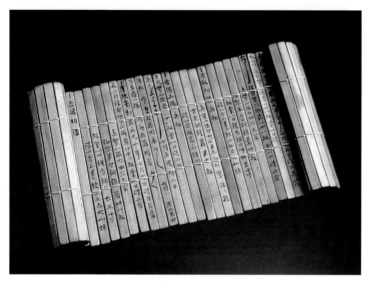

A book with words written on bamboo slips. It is identified as belonging to the eighth century BC.

Influence of Chinese on the cultural development of Japan, Korea and Vietnam was also strong. Ancient Japanese, Koreans and Vietnamese borrowed Chinese characters to record things in their own languages. Chinese characters are no longer used in modern Korean and Vietnamese languages. In 1981, Japan published a list of 1,954 Chinese characters that are most active in Japanese.

Papermaking and Printing

Chinese characters in their earliest form were cut on bones and tortoise shells, and then on bronze artifacts. In the Spring and Autumn period, bamboo slips and silk cloth came to be used as writing materials. It was certainly easier to write with brushes on bamboo slips or silk cloth. The problem was that silk cloth was too expensive and that bamboo slips were too heavy. In other words, neither material was good enough for practical use. A ranking official under Emperor Wu Di of the Han Dynasty once wrote a report to his majesty. The "report", so to speak, turned out to be stacks of 3,000 bamboo slips that had to be carried into the emperor's office.

According to historic records and archeological finds, the Chinese

Illustration in a Ming Dynasty (1368-1644) book, showing workers preparing bamboo plants for making paper pulp with.

of the West Han period were already producing paper — paper so crude that could only be used for packaging. In the year 105 AD, Cai Lun improved the papermaking techniques, and the kind of paper he produced by using tree barks, rags, hemp fibers and discarded fishing nets as raw materials was not only good for writing on but was also cost effective. By the 4th century, paper had become the major writing material and, thanks to widespread use of writing paper, calligraphy became able to develop as an art form.

And about the same time, papermaking was introduced to Korea, and then to Vietnam, Japan and India. In the 8th century, the Arabs learned papermaking techniques from the Chinese. Tang Dynasty soldiers, who had worked at paper mills before they fought to what is now Iran, built the first paper mill outside China and, as time went by, paper replaced parchment that was much more expensive. Then, in the 11th century, the Arabs brought papermaking techniques to Europe.

Use of paper ushered in a flourishing publishing industry. For circulation, books had had to be reproduced by hand copying before paper was invented — a time and labor consuming process in which errors and mistakes were frequent occurences. In 8th century (or in the 7th as some scholars insist), the Chinese invented the art of printing. It was, in fact, wood block printing. The text to be printed was first written on a sheet of thin, translucent paper, which was glued face downward on the plate. The characters were then carved out in relief with a knife. For printing, the engraved plate with carved characters in the negative was inked, and then a sheet of paper was spread over it. By brushing the paper gently and evenly, the characters in the positive were imprinted on it. Lots of Buddhist scripts and classics of Confucianism were printed under the auspices of the government or by private citizens. Private printing shops, which were operating for a profit, mushroomed, and collections of poetry, almanacs and textbooks became available on the open market. An exquisitely printed volume of *Diamond Sutra,* which was found in 1900 in one of Dunhuang grottoes, bears the date of its production: the "fifteenth day of the fourth moon in the ninth year of Xiantong (868 AD)". The volume, now in the collection of the London Museum of Great Britain, is the world's earliest known printed work that bears the exact date of production.

Block printing had an enormous advantage over hand copying, as by using one plate, the text could be reproduced again and again. The carving of the plate, however, was a difficult task. Then in the mid-

Moveable printing types of baked clay in an iron frame.

11th century, Bi Sheng developed the art of movable type printing. The process started with making of clay types, one for each character. The types were fired for hardness. The hard clay types were circumscribed with an iron frame, and a layer of resin was spread on the bottom of the frame. A plate of types would be ready when the frames were full. Then the plate was heated over a fire until the clay types turned into pottery types. For higher efficiency two iron sheets were used, one for fresh typesetting and the other for printing. After printing, the types were taken off the plate for re-use.

This process, known as "movable type printing", consists of the same three elements of modern type printing — type making, typesetting and printing. It was simple and efficient relative to block printing. Moreover, the types were easy to use and preserve. By following the same principle, the Chinese after Bi Sheng invented printing with movable types of wood, bronze or tin. In the 13th century, movable type printing was introduced to Korea, and from Korea, the art spread to Japan, Vietnam and Central Asia.

1. Xixia (1038-1227) was a political regime set up by the Qiang ethnic group during the Song Dynasty. During its heyday, the regime administered an area encompassing parts of what are now Ningxia, Gansu, Qinghai and Inner Mongolia.

Silk, Wine, Tea and Porcelain

China, the Land of Silk

Among all peoples in the world, the Chinese are the first to have engaged in sericulture and production of silk textiles. Fragments of silkworm cocoons and silk cloth, motifs of silkworms on pottery ware, and spindles of various shapes that have been unearthed so far all lead to the conclusion that in China, sericulture and textile production date to five or six thousand years ago. Moreover, silk and silk textiles were already used for exchange on the market in times of remote antiquity. According to inscriptions on a bronze vessel of the West Zhou, a horse, plus a bundle of silk, could be traded for five slaves.

In traditional Chinese families, men had the duty to work the fields while women stayed indoor to do spinning. This way of life – a life

Sericulture (partial), from a Song Dynasty (960-1279) book.

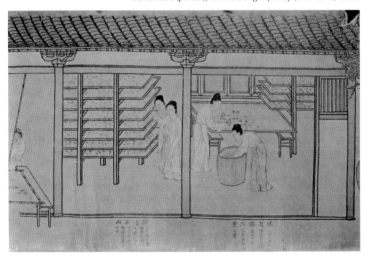

of self-sufficiency — is vividly depicted in numerous traditional Chinese paintings, folk paintings in particular. But still more important are those beautiful pieces done by ancient weaving maids that have been preserved to this day. From a tomb on the outskirts of Changsha, Hunan Province, that belongs to a Chu noblewoman of the Warring States period, archeologists found a stack of two dozen pieces of silk textiles, mostly pieces of brocade. Though more than 2,000 years old, these are still bright in color and the patterns on them are still discernible. In the Song Dynasty, areas south of the Yangtze River were better developed than areas north of the river in silk textile production. The Lake Taihu Basin on the lower reaches of the Yangtze and Sichuan on the upper reaches of the river were the most important producing areas, but Sichuan products were rated as the best. The dynasty had an imperial textile mill in its capital Bianliang (what is now Kaifeng, Henan Province), where craftsmen from Sichuan worked day in and day out to produce for the imperial family and high-ranking officials. In ancient China, silk cloth was meant for a privileged few, while clothing of inferior materials was for the laboring masses. Here are lines from a Tang Dynasty poem

A piece of Tang Dynasty (618-907) brocade. It was discovered in Turpan of Xinjiang, a hub of communication on the ancient Silk Road.

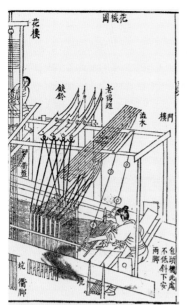

Illustrations from a Ming Dynasty (960-1279) book on science and engineering: the structure of a jacquard weaving machine (left) and a workman processing natural silk (right).

protesting against this unfairness:

> Of those covered by silk all over
> None has had any experience in silkworm raising.

China began exporting silk and silk textiles in the Han Dynasty. The dynasty opened those trading routes that snaked westward to states in central and west Asia. An office was set up to administer affairs related to the West Region, which also had the task of ensuring safety of travelling merchants and providing them with food, water and other necessities. Trains of horses and camels carrying silk and silk textiles started from Chang'an (what is now Xi'an, Shaanxi Province), and made their way westward through the Gansu corridor and across the vast Gobi desert in Xinjiang to West Asia and then further west to Europe. Silk conquered the ancient Romans, and they chose to called China "Serice" — meaning the "land of silk". Lucius Julius Caesar (?-87 BC) caused no small a sensation when he made a public appearance in a silk robe. And before long, wearing silk clothes became a high-class fashion.

The trading routes linking ancient China with Africa, West Asia and Europe, plus sea routes that were opened later, are referred to as the Silk Road. The Silk Road is seen as the symbol of cultural intercourse and trade between the East and the West in ancient times. For well over 2,000 years, the Silk Road made it possible for the West to benefit from ancient Chinese civilization highlighted by silk, porcelain and papermaking, and for ancient China to enrich its culture with goods, production techniques, musical instruments and religions from faraway countries.

The ancient Chinese were also the first to grow hemp, and among the first to grow cotton. Fujian, the Hainan Island and parts of northwest China used to be the main cotton producing areas and, by the 12th or 13th century, the cash crop had come to be grown in the north and most parts of south China. The Ming Dynasty, in particular, allowed tax exemption to cotton growers to encourage higher output. As time went by, cotton cloth replaced silk and linen as the main material of clothing for the Chinese.

Clothing of Ancient Chinese

Clothing of ancient Chinese varied from dynasty to dynasty and from ethnic group to ethnic group. But generally speaking, garments worn by people living south of the Great Wall had the fronts in the right, while garments worn by people living north of the Great Wall had the fronts in the left. For the sake of horsemanship and archery, nomads living in China's far north wore short-sleeved jackets, long trousers and leather boots. These nomads were referred to as *Hu*, and their costumes were called *Hu fu*, or the *Hu* clothing. In the prolonged process of cultural intercourse, the Han majority and people of the various ethnic minority groups were able to share each other's style of clothing. A striking example is clothing of the Tang Dynasty, which in many ways resembled clothing of those nomadic tribes. An even earlier example is the State of Zhao of the Warring States Period, whose rulers ordered adoption of clothing in *Hu* style,

Tang Dynasty (618-907) tricolor figurine of a man from central or west Asia.

on the ground that short-slaved and close-fit, *Hu* clothing was more suitable for combating and military training.

Though diverse in style, ancient Chinese clothing consisted of two basic parts, *yi,* the upper garment and *shang*, the lower garment. *Shang* in its earliest form consisted of two pieces of cloth tied to the front and rear of the lower part of the body. People of the Han Dynasty sewed the pieces for *qun* — something like culottes, and *qun* was also worn by for both men and women of the following dynasties. Then came *shen yi* produced by sewing *yi* and *shang* together, and on the basis of *shen yi* that traditional robes were developed. Laborers wore shorts, or *duan da* as known to the Chinese. Long robes, however, were for aristocrats, officials and scholars. *Duan da* and long robes were the basic forms of clothing throughout the feudal times, though there were variations in size and pattern.

In feudal China, the ethnical code of Confucianism manifested itself in everything, and the ways people were dressed were clearly distinctive of their differences in social status. All dynasties had a set of rules specifying every minute detail of clothing worn by people of each class or social strata, ranging from the style, pattern and materials of the clothes and hats to the kind of ornaments people were allowed to use. Silk cloth was reserved for ranking officials

Tricolor glazed pottery female figurines,
of the Tang Dynasty (618-907).

and aristocrats. In ancient Chinese vocabulary, "*bu yi*" (cotton
clothes) and "*bai xing*" (commoners) were synonyms. In the Han
Dynasty, red was the color for aristocrats, and in the Tang, purple.
From the Tang Dynasty to the Qing, yellow was meant exclusive for
emperors and their direct relatives, and the colors of commoners'
clothing were limited to blue, white and black. And for this reason,
persons with neither official nor aristocratic titles were often referred
to as *bai yi*, which literally means "persons wearing white clothes".
Ranks and status were often indicated in patterns on clothes. The
Dragon pattern was meant for emperors exclusively. Official gowns
of the Qing Dynasty had embroidered patches on the chest and the
back, and on the patches there were designs of different birds and
animals to denote the different ranks of the wearers. Generally
speaking, patterns of legendary or real birds were embroidered on
patches for civilian officials, and military officials were entitled to
fierce-looking animals either real or legendary.

All dynasties forbade overstepping of one's rank by wearing clothes one was not entitled to. Under the *Criminal and Civil Code of the Ming Dynasty*, a commoner would be given 50 lashes for wearing clothes meant for officials, and an official would be flogged 100 times for wearing clothes for ranks higher than his own. Throughout the history of feudal China, there were numerous cases in which people were executed for using the dragon design. It is true that there were changes to the styles of clothing from time to time. Nevertheless, clothing was always an embodiment of the system of hierarchy.

Despite that, folkways constantly changed and so did social conditions, hence the imprints of different cultures and times on clothes worn by the Chinese. Society of the Tang Dynasty was relatively open or liberal. This emboldened women to go against the tradition and wear dresses that were loose enough to expose the upper part of their chests, and some women were even courageous enough to wear men's clothing. By tradition, ancient Han Chinese, men and women alike, wore their hair in a bun on the head. The Qing Dynasty forced the ethnic Hans to adopt the mandarin hairstyle and clothing. So men all had the crowns of their heads shaven with pigtails hanging from the back of their heads, and their formal dresses were mandarin jackets worn over gowns. In the 1920s, *qi pao,* an improved model of the mandarin female gown that features high neck and slit skirt became fashionable all over China. After the Qing was toppled, a tight collar tunic suit (sometimes referred to as the "Mao suit" in recent decades) modeled after Japanese student uniform became the standard dress for men. As Western influence grows, more and more Chinese have shifted to Western suits over the past century.

Chinese Cuisine

In some of the Silk Road remains, archeologists have found dumplings and *nang* (a kind of crusty pancake) they believe to have left over from the Tang Dynasty. The discovery instantly aroused scholarly attention, as it reinforces the belief that one has to know

The photo shows Empress Dowager Ci Xi (center, 1835-1908), *de facto* ruler of China in the late Qing period, with a bevy of court ladies. Note the Manchurian costumes, which differentiate the rankings of the wearers.

something about Chinese cuisine in order to appreciate the Chinese culture.

The Chinese diet began diversifying in times of remote antiquity. Ever since the Han Dynasty, cooked wheaten food has been the main diet for people living in areas north of the Qinling Mountains and the Huaihe River, where wheat and foxtail millet are the main crops. Rice has been the main staple for people in the south, where plenty of rain and warm weather are suitable for growth of the rice crop. In comparison, nomads on the Qinghai-Tibet Plateau in the northwest and on grasslands in the far north have always lived on meat and cheese. Chinese food is recognized as most diverse in variety. With wheat flour and rice, for example, the Chinese can, by using methods of streaming, boiling, baking, frying, etc., produce staples such as steamed rice, steamed bread, dumplings and noodles, as well as snacks in hundreds of varieties with distinct local flavor. Rice and wheat flour are called *xi liang* or "fine food grain", relative to *cu liang* — "coarse food grain" — like millet, sorghum, maize, etc. "Coarse"? Maybe. But staples and snacks made of "coarse grain" are equally delicious. Among the countless Chinese dishes, more than 1,000 are recognized as the best examples of the Chinese cuisine. It is safe to assert that no gourmet, however seasoned, can claim to have tried dishes of all Chinese cuisine schools.

Cooking of Chinese food is an art in itself. It is the art of cutting and slicing, the art of choosing the right materials for a dish, and the art of using the cooking fire in such a way as to ensure that all ingredients, no matter how diverse, are properly done. Indeed, a good dish is a fine piece of artwork, a perfect combination of color, taste and flavor while the different ingredients are artistically arranged. A good chef can cut something like a radish into a beautiful flower, a life-like fish, etc. A formal dinner invariably turns out to be a feast to the eye as well, with dishes that not only tastes good but also feature a unique artistic style. The principle of melting color, flavor and taste together is followed even in preparing homely food.

Chinese in different regions of the country have developed different schools of cuisine, each being distinctive of the natural resources, climate, diet habits and tradition of the region where it originates. The Sichuan, Guangdong, Shandong and Huiyang schools are the most popular or the most important.

Sichuan food, which originates from the Sichuan Basin in southwest China, has so many varieties that to exhaust all dishes of the school, you may keep trying a new dish at each and every meal for a whole year. Sichuan food is hot and spicy with a lot of pepper and chili. It is damp and foggy most of the days in the Sichuan Basin, prompting the popular belief that hot, spicy food helps people keep fit. And thanks to the unique taste of

Pastries found in Turpan, Xinjiang. These should be food for travelers on the Silk Road.

the food, Sichuan has always been referred to as the "paradise for eaters".

Dishes of the Guangdong school have two salient features: a large choice of materials and preference to things live and fresh to cook with such as fish and seafood fresh from water. It is hot in subtropical south China where the Guangdong school of cuisine originates. As food is easy to perish there, people are naturally keen to the freshness of food and, as time goes by, have developed a special liking for things cooked tender — so tender that cooked food still retains the original taste and flavor of seafood, freshwater fish, vegetables, etc. Guangzhou, the center of south China, has been a trading port since ancient times, and chefs there have had to cater to tastes of people from different parts of the world, hence the large choice of materials for dishes of the Guandgong cuisine.

The Huaiyang school originates from Yangzhou in Jiangsu Province, east China, which incorporates what is the best in food popular in the Huai'an area and other parts of northern Jiangsu, hence the name "Huaiyang". In ancient times, Yangzhou in the middle of the Grand Canal, the country's major north-south waterway, was a thriving economic and cultural center and, as such, it was an ideal venue for gatherings of high-ranking officials, scholars, poets, and rich merchants. It is against this background that the art of Huaiyang cooking was developed and has been passed down to this day, an art that features not only delicious taste of dishes but also an urbane, elegant cultural atmosphere at dinners or banquets.

High caloric, high protein materials — meat, for example — constitute a salient feature of dishes that originate from Shandong, northern China. This may be attributed to the fact that northern China, of which Shandong is a part, is colder than areas in the south and, therefore, vegetables available there are in fewer varieties and smaller quantities. In ancient times, Shandong dishes were an important part of the imperial menu, including, for example, the famous Beijing roast duck. The Shandong school of cuisine is famous for roast meat and instant-boiled mutton slices. Obviously, these dishes originated

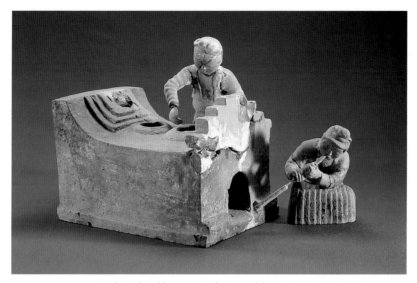

Female cook and her assistant, figurines of the Sui Dynasty (581-618).

from areas inhabited by nomadic tribes in China's far north.

The Chinese use chopsticks for eating. But still more representative of the Chinese culture is the ceremony and propriety that are related to eating. At a formal dinner, participants are seated in order of seniority for age and position, and how close a host is related to the host is also taken into account in arranging the seating. When the dinner is ready, nobody would touch the food without a gesture of invitation from the most senior male member of the host family. Moreover, a special ritual of courtesy has to be followed in proposing toasts or presenting the guests with tea. Rules of this kind are no longer strictly followed in many modern Chinese families, but practically all families will feast on the eve of the Spring Festival or the Moon Festival to celebrate a joyous reunion.

Alcoholic Beverages and the Inner World of the Chinese

Archeologists have found large numbers of ancient wine vessels, as well as remains of ancient wineries, proving that China was already producing alcoholic beverages about 5,000 years ago. In 1979, two bottles of wine, identified as belonging to the Warring States period more than 2,000 years ago, were unearthed in Pingshan County, Hebei Province. A sweet smell characteristic of wines fresh from the winery assailed the nostrils immediately after the bottles were opened. The superb quality of the ancient wine and its alcoholic content are sufficient to explain everything, though the airtight containers may also have played a role in preserving the beverage.

In the year 98 AD, the Han Dynasty decreed government monopoly of wine production and marketing, but some years afterwards people were again allowed to produce and sell alcoholic beverages provided they paid taxes to the government. This may suggest that China under the Han Dynasty had a fairly developed wine brewery industry, and that the industry was profitable. In the Han and all the succeeding dynasties, wine production, along with iron smelting, was a major source of the state revenue. But governments may ban wine production in times of famine or war when food grains were in short supply.

Before the Tang Dynasty, the Chinese consumed either undecanted wine or "pressed wine" – alcoholic liquid produced by pressing or filtering the fermented brewing materials. The yellow wine, a low-alcohol pressed wine produced with glutinous rice or millet as raw material, was the earliest Chinese wine and is still a special Chinese product.

As time went by, liquor replaced wine as the main alcoholic drink consumed by the Chinese. Liquor, which is produced by distilling, is much stronger. In liquor production, anything rich in starch and sugar can be used for fermentation – food grains, potatoes and wild plants alike, but sorghum liquor is the best. Maotai produced in Guizhou Province, southwest China, is known as the "state liquor" for its use at state banquets but still more for its popularity. Here is the saying about the superb liquor that has been in production for more than 460 years: open a bottle of Maotai and the sweet smell is so strong that people get tipsy even before drinking the liquor. China produces liquor in countless varieties. Of these, famous brands like

Maotai each have a unique taste and flavor.

In ancient China, wineries and distilleries were found in all cities and towns. In the countryside, almost all families produced glutinous rice wine for their own consumption, mainly on festival occasions and at parties. In some places families would, by following the tradition, make some rice wine when a daughter was born. The wine was not for immediate consumption, but was kept in airtight jars for use at the girl's wedding party many years later. The "maiden wine", so to speak, would be exceptionally good, as it had been stored for a long time. Homemade alcoholic drinks popular among people of China's ethnic minority groups are unique in taste and flavor. A guest in a Mongolian yurt is always invited to drink, to his or her heart's content, an alcoholic beverage produced through fermentation of mare's milk. The "mare's milk wine", so to speak, tastes a bit sour and is very refreshing. As regards the Tibetans, offering a large bowl of highland barley wine is the way of welcoming in a guest.

Wines and liquors have been a part of the Chinese culture – in fact an indispensable part of people's life. Ever since ancient times, there have been numerous poems and essays about how people express their feelings or aspirations in wines and liquors. Here is a quotation from an essay by Ouyang Xiu, a Song Dynasty poet, writer and statesman: "The delight

Bronze *jue*, a wine vessel of the Shang period (16th century BC-11th century BC).

of the Old Tippler (the author) does not reside in wine. The joy of mountains and rivers he holds in his heart is expressed in wine."

Cao Cao (155-220), a top statesman and strategist of the Three Kingdoms period, wrote of his resolve to defy old age and fulfill his political ambitions in a poem that begins with these lines:

Cup to cup calls the song; Man's life —for how long?
A morning's dew? Alas, many a day is done.

A Tang Dynasty poem describes how a soldier sees wars:

Don't laugh at my laying on the battle ground in a drunken stupor;
Of the soldiers in wars since ancient times
How many have returned safe and sound?

Ancient Chinese poets took a special liking for drinking, from which they drew so much inspiration. The best example was Li Bai (701-762), a Tang Dynasty poet of romanticism, who had the nickname "sage with a bottle" for relying on wine for inspiration while known as the "God of poetry" for his accomplishments in poetry. Here is a rough translation of a poem by Du Fu (712-770), a contemporary poet, in praise of Li Bai:

With a flagon of wine Li Bai produces a hundred poems;
In a drunken stupor, he lays in a Chang'an wine shop in dreams.
An invitation from the emperor? No, your majesty
In wine your humble servant is a deity.

The importance of wines and liquors is manifest in every aspect of the Chinese folkways. Sacrificial ceremonies, weddings, birthday parties, burials, etc. without wines or liquors would be simply unthinkable. When friends or relatives meet for dining, for enhanced joyous mood *jiu ling* or drinkers' wager games are often played. Under the auspices of a referee — normally one who does not drink — participants take turns to take quizzes or compose poems on the rhyme ordered by the referee, and those who fail in the game will be made to drink as a forfeit.

At banquets, toasts are invariably exchanged between participants to express their best wishes for one another. Meanwhile, those who commit a breach of etiquette will be made to drink a forfeit, hence

Han Xizai at a Night Feast, a painting of the Five Dynasties period (907-960). Han, a high-ranking official, had some serious grudges with the emperor. To protect himself, he deliberately put himself in the world of wine and women to convince the suspicious sovereign that he had no political ambition.

the saying "refuse a toast only to drink a forfeit" — meaning submitting to a person's pressure after first turning down the person's request. But don't imagine that the Chinese are drunkards. In fact the Chinese hold in contempt those who are unbridled in drinking and do silly things under the influence of alcohol, calling them *jiu gui* (devil drunkards). In the eyes of the Chinese, a "good drinker" is one who expresses his ideals and feelings or demonstrates his wisdom and talent by way of drinking. The Chinese stand for *jiu de* or propriety in drinking, the essence of which is summarized as "be sober minded when all others are drunken".

Tea and its Cultural Connotations

China is the country of tea, the country where tea growing, processing of fresh tealeaves and tea drinking originate. *Cha Jing* or the *Canon of Tea* by Lu Yu of the 8th century is the world's earliest book on tea. It is in fact an encyclopaedia of tea — the origin of tea

Tea Party on Mt. Huishan, a Ming Dynasty (960-1279) painting, depicts scholars enjoying tea and natural scenery while meeting new friends.

shrubs and their cultivation, plucking and processing of tealeaves, ways of preparing tea, and the ritual for tea drinking. No wonder its importance to studies of tea cultivation and production in China and the world.

Back in the early Han Dynasty tea was already consumed as a daily necessity. Tea is among those burial objects excavated from a West Han (c. 206 BC-25 BC) tomb at Mawangdui on the outskirts of Changsha, Hunan Province, testifying to the importance of tea to people's life. By the period of the North and South Dynasties, a ritual had been developed in southern China that called for presenting tea as a gesture of courtesy or respect. In the 9th century, tea cultivation was brought to Japan along with tea drinking, and then to other countries in the following centuries.

An old saying goes something like this: Families need seven things to survive — firewood, rice, cooking oil, salt, sauce, vinegar and tea, meaning that tea is as essential to the Chinese as food. And for its importance, tea business became a major source of the state revenue under China's feudal dynasties. Beginning as of the Tang

Dynasty, governments imposed a tea tax and set up government-run tea gardens in effort to monopolize tea trading. Tea grows in areas on the middle and lower reaches of the Yangtze River and in parts of southwest China. Horses, however, were produced mainly in the north. The Song Dynasty traded tea for battle steeds with nomadic tribes to the benefit of both parties. The dynasty badly needed horses for defense. Without drinking much tea to stimulate digestion, the nomads, who lived mainly on meat and milk, would find life too hard to bear.

While quenching thirst, tea, with a cocaine content, is refreshing. Many Chinese are addicted to tea. As the old saying goes, tea addicts "would rather give up wine for life than not to have tea just for one day". Ancient Chinese developed a set of rules governing everything for a tea party, ranging from the kind of tea things to be used, the ways tea was to be prepared, the way the tea room was to be decorated, to the ceremony and propriety that participants were to follow. Such rules eventually died out in China. In Japan, however, the same rules developed into *chado* or the "tea ceremony" — an elaborate process that features courtesy and elegance.

Teahouses are found all over China, and are always crowded with customers — again proving the popularity of tea drinking. Beijing, Suzhou, Guangdong and Sichuan are best known for teahouses. While drinking tea, customers in teahouses in Beijing may enjoy story telling or ballad singing performed on a small stage. Enjoyment over tea and, at the same time, over scenery motivates people to go to teahouses in Suzhou, a most picturesque city with numerous waterways and private gardens. Nationwide, teahouses of the Suzhou type outnumber those of any other type. Teahouses in Guangdong serve food as well, where "tea drinking" often turns out to be a feast of snacks in scores of varieties. Now a regular part of life in Guangdong, this phenomenon was, however, a legacy of history dating to the Tang-Song period when merchants customarily met in teahouses to discuss business. Teahouses in Sichuan, mostly with

A modern teahouse. Note the customers sipping tea while enjoying ballad singing.

Rubbings of North Song Dynasty (960-1127) relieves, showing a woman washing tea things (left) and another making tea (right).

simple furnishing, afford an easy atmosphere, where customers pay a little money for tea while enjoying themselves over gossip and mahjong. "Society in miniature" — that's how Sichuan teahouses are sometimes called.

People of letters and refined scholars have had their own ways of tea drinking, ways of pursuing urbanity and elegance. They gather in tastefully decorated rooms for tea parties, and the tea they are served is always made of top quality leaves and pure spring water. Temperamentally compatible, the host and guests exchange poems in the course of such a tea party — normally the host writing a poem and the guests each writing one in reply, using the same rhyme scheme. There are also tea parties at which calligraphic works or paintings in the hosts' collection are displayed and participants are invited to comment. Everybody else will be offended if a guest does or speak silly things that spoil the atmosphere. Meat dishes are a taboo, as tea parties are meant to let attendants enjoy the pure, sweet fragrance of tea.

The Country of Porcelain

China is reputed not only for porcelain tableware, tea sets, drinking sets and stationary but also for porcelain art pieces modeled after human figures, plants and animals. Like silk, porcelain articles have always been important export commodities of the country. Marine

Tricolor glazed pottery steed of
the Tang Dynasty (618-907).

archeologists have found numerous Chinese porcelain articles or
broken pieces in salvaged ships that sank in ancient times. Moreover,
ancient Chinese porcelain art objects are found in numerous museum
collections across the world.

Porcelain was developed on the basis of steady improvements in
pottery-making techniques. As far as 7,000 or 8,000 years ago,
China's primitive residents were already producing pottery bowls,
jars, vases, and pots. By the Qin-Han period about 2,000 years ago,
production of earthenware, in both output and quality, had reached
an unprecedented high level. Pottery artifacts of this period feature
prominently in the history of traditional Chinese art. Among these,
the Qin Dynasty "army" of life-size terra cotta soldiers, battle steeds
and war chariots supposedly to guard the mausoleum of China's first
emperor, Emperor Shi Huang, dazzle the world with their artistic
magnificence, and so did those Han Dynasty figurines of story tellers,
musicians and acrobats. The trio-colored glazed pottery of the Tang
Dynasty represented a new height in the development of ancient

China's pottery art, the most brilliant of these being human, horse and camel figurines.

Celadon artifacts unearthed from remains of the Shang period are identified as the earliest porcelain ever produced in China. But due to insufficient attention to selection of materials and use of primitive firing techniques in production, the layer of glaze on the surface of this kind of porcelain is not even and fast enough. And for this reason, primitive celadons are called "proto-porcelain". About 1,000 years after primitive celadons or proto-porcelain ware came into being, that is, during the East Han period, the Chinese succeeded in producing celadon pieces that were good enough to meet every standard for genuine porcelain.

Ming Dynasty (960-1279) porcelain jar with a lid, with design of fish and algae.

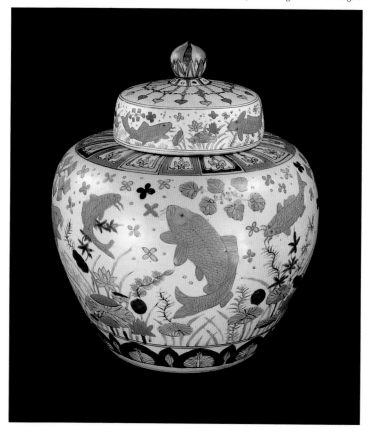

Yuan Dynasty (1271-1368) jar with a lid, with dragon design in red.

The Tang Dynasty made all-round improvements in porcelain-making techniques and set up a network of porcelain kilns that were named after the places where they were built. Celadons were produced mainly in areas south of then Yangtze River with what is now Zhejiang as center, and what is now Hebei Province in north China was the production center of white porcelain. But until now, pure and painted white porcelain utensils and art artifacts have been in most widespread use in the country.

The Song Dynasty witnessed breakthroughs in porcelain-making techniques. Porcelain products became diversified in style and variety while output kept increasing, indicating that gone was the period of "white-in-north-and-greenish-in-south" – a Tang Dynasty pet phase referring to the main varieties of Chinese porcelain and distribution of their production. Porcelain kilns sprang up everywhere, including some 30 rated as most important. But products of the Ding, Jun, Ge, Ru and Guan kilns[1], the "greatest five", are always most valued for their artistic and historic importance. It is also during the Song period that China began exporting porcelain ware in large quantities.

Porcelain production experienced a golden age in the Song and the following dynasties, during which period the output kept growing, techniques improving and products increasing in variety. In the Ming Dynasty, Jingdezhen, Jiangxi Province, became the country's "porcelain capital", the producer of the country's most beautiful, most refined porcelain ware. Blue and white porcelain ware were the mainstream products of the Ming Dynasty – porcelain ware coated with a thin layer of fine white glaze while pictures of scenery, birds or animals are painted in blue.

Chinese porcelain techniques reached their peak in development from the mid-17th century to the end of 18th, and products became even more diverse in style, color and design. The "porcelain capital", Jingdezhen, received still greater support from the court, where more than 100,000 artists and craftsmen were working during its heyday. The first few emperors of the Qing Dynasty were especially interested

Qing Dynasty (1644-1911) vat, with design pure blue in color that depicts the Pavilion of Prince Teng at the side of the Dongting Lake.

in porcelain. Under their reigns, officials were appointed to supervise over porcelain production and court painters were ordered to help design porcelain ware for the imperial collection. Emperor Qian Long, in particular, even personally took up porcelain design and production. Porcelain articles of the Qing period are of a still more decorative value, with the themes of paintings on them never so diverse. Traditional themes – flowers, birds, insects and fish – were retained. Meanwhile, new themes were adopted, including for example complete paintings of scenery and human figures and paintings based on stories from classical Chinese novels or traditional operas.

From the Song Dynasty through to the Qing, there were *guan yao* or "government kilns" producing exclusively to meet imperial needs. These kilns had a limited output and, for quality and style, never cared about the costs. Products from non-government kilns fell into two types – those for the high-class and those for the lower classes. But no matter who the producers were, porcelain artifacts left over from that period are highly valued as museum pieces or pieces in private collections.

1. Of the five "greatest porcelain kilns" of the Song Dynasty, Ding, Jun, Ge, and Ru are, separately, in what is now Quyang County, Hebei province; Yuxian County of Henan Province; Longquan of Zhejiang Province; and Linru County of Henan Province. Remains of the Guan Kilns are yet to be found though historic records and relics are sufficient to prove their existence.

China's Architectural Art

Characteristics of Traditional Chinese Architecture

In style and structure, ancient Chinese architecture is distinctively different from structures of Western architectural schools.

Most ancient buildings found in the West are stone structures. In comparison, ancient Chinese buildings are mostly of a wooden frame structure, and even buildings of masonry - Buddhist pagodas, palace buildings, mausoleums, etc. - have an exterior modeled after wooden frame structures. The upright columns, not the walls, are the supporting parts of such buildings, hence the old saying, "Walls may collapse, houses — never." By adopting the wooden frame structure, the Chinese have been able to build the outer and inner walls of a building in ways that best suit local conditions. In north China where it is cold, structures normally have thick, solid walls. In south China

Traditional wooden structures feature halls, chambers and pavilions without walls.

where it is hot, walls of houses are often built with wooden boards or woven bamboo mats, and there are even structures without walls, such as *ting* (pavilions), *xie* (pavilions on terraces), *lang* (corridors), as well as some of the halls. Moreover, a large room may easily be partitioned into chambers with boards or screens. Buildings of wooden frame structure are easy to construct and relatively earthquake-proof, but are not as strong as stone structures. Few ancient buildings of wooden frame structure have remained intact to this day because timber is easy to burn and become moth-eaten and decomposed.

Ancient Chinese buildings are always in neat clusters that are surrounded by walls, whether they are palace buildings, monasteries or just ordinary residential buildings. A single building in a group may not be so large as a church or a house in the West, but buildings walled as a group or cluster invariably look imposing. Except those serving special purposes like watchtowers on city walls and bell and drum towers that told time in ancient times, separate building in traditional Chinese style seldom fully expose their contours, and therefore it is difficult for people to have a full view of them from a distance. Because of this, to fully appreciate the beauty of a single building one often needs to seek a full view of the group or cluster of which it is one.

A group of ancient Chinese buildings normally form a neat square, with the left and right rows of buildings facing each other in symmetric order. The courtyard occupies the central part of the walled square. If the courtyard is large, pains will be taken to arrange the buildings in such a way as to ensure a perfect axial symmetry. In ancient times, this principle was followed even in planning the layout of streets and buildings in a city. As is still discernible in any ancient Chinese city, the largest and most imposing group of buildings always occupies the most prominent place — the center of the axis that runs through the city's symmetric length. In comparison, much more freedom was allowed to designing of gardens. Pavilions, halls and other buildings in a garden always form an integral whole, but they

The Long Corridor in the Summer Palace, Beijing, with color pictures painted on the beams. The pictures are based on legends or stories told in classical Chinese novels or traditional operas.

are arranged in such a way as to fit in with the natural topography of the surrounding.

When building a structure, ancient Chinese always worked painstakingly to make everything in its exterior — even those eaves tiles — highly decorative. The roof of a typical ancient building is, in fact, an elaborate system of wooden beams and purlins and, as such, it may look heavy. But in no way does it look clumsy as the four tips curve up. Moreover, the various construction members of the ridgepole are invariably in the shape of small animals, and floral and animal designs are carved even on those tile-ends, making the entire building look enchanting. To prolong the life of a building, ancient Chinese invariably painted the exposed parts of the wooden structures. As time went by, *cai hua* or decorative paintings done on eaves came into being as an indepndent branch of the traditional

Chinese fine art.

Ancient Chinese architecture can be classified into palace buildings, mausoleums, religious buildings, ritual buildings, gardens and residential buildings.

Palace Buildings

Palace buildings were meant exclusive for emperors and their families. No wonder these are the most imposing and the best in construction quality. In comparison, in many other countries it is temples, churches and other religious shrines that represent the highest achievements of ancient architecture.

An ancient Chinese palace complex consists of individual buildings in neat groups that are placed according to a certain order. The main buildings always sit astride the north-south axis of the palace complex, and to the left and right of the main buildings lie less important buildings. The main hall, where the emperor handled state affairs, always occupies the frontal section of the palace complex, and the imperial family's living quarters and the imperial gardens are in the rear section. Surrounded by walls, the palace complex is, in fact, a "city" in itself - the "imperial city" within the country's capital city. In ancient times, the "imperial city" featured most prominently in the capital city - in its very center, as a matter of fact. Also occupying the most prominent parts of the capital city were altars dedicated to the Heaven and Earth in whose name the emperor ruled, as

Gates in the Forbidden City.

The Forbidden City, the largest and the best-preserved imperial palace complex in the world.

well as the temple where the imperial family's ancestors were worshipped. And far beyond the walls of the "imperial city" were market places, streets and residential areas. To sum up, monarchical supremacy and order characterized the designing and development of the capital city of any feudal dynasty. In other words, this was the rule that all feudal dynasties followed in constructing their capital cities.

The Forbidden City in Beijing is the largest and the best preserved imperial palace complex in the world. Construction of the Forbidden City began in 1407 and was completed 1420. The Forbidden City was home to 24 emperors of China's last two dynasties, the Ming and the Qing that ruled China for 490 years. Walls that total three kilometers in length surround the Forbidden City. There are four main gates facing south, north, east and west. Atop each gate there is a watchtower and at each corner of the wall there is a turret. And round the walls flows the imperial moat. The Hall of Supreme Harmony, the Hall of Midway Harmony and the Hall of Perfect Harmony are in the frontal section of the Forbidden City. Of these, the most important - certainly the most magnificent - is the Hall of Supreme Harmony. This was the venue for imperial audience and

The Hall of Supreme Harmony, the most
important structure in the Forbidden City.

the most important ceremonies such as those for assumption of the
throne by a new emperor, celebration of the emperors' birthdays and
weddings, and announcement of imperial edicts. The most important
festivals, the Spring Festival and the Moon Festival, were also
celebrated in the hall, when ministers and generals made obeisance
to the country's supreme ruler. The rear section of the Forbidden
City was where the emperors and his wives and children lived, but
there are also chambers where the emperor handled routine affairs
of court administration.

The ground plan and architectural style of the Forbidden City are
a concentrated expression of the ancient Chinese culture characteristic
of a stringent hierarchical system with attention paid to every minute
detail to stress the supremacy of the monarchical power. The main
buildings stand in a neat row astride the axis of the walled complex.
The Hall of Supreme Harmony, the largest and the most imposing of
all buildings in the palace complex, is placed in the center of the
frontal section. Five gates pierce the Meridian Gate, the main gate
for the inner part of the Forbidden City. The gate in the middle was
reserved for the emperor, and the other gates, separately for ministers,
generals, princes and princesses and successful candidates in the

highest imperial examinations. The studs on the gates of the Forbidden City are also symbols of monarchical power. In the Ming Dynasty, gates of the Forbidden City were painted in bright red with 81 golden studs on each that were arranged in nine rows. Officials, however, must have their gates painted in green or black according to their rankings, with 25 studs in color of bronze or iron. Princes living outside the Forbidden City may have their gates painted in red and the studs in golden yellow. But there is a difference: they were allowed to have 49 studs in seven rows on a gate. The ground plan and construction style of the imperial city were meant for the emperor and his family only, and no one outside the imperial family was allowed to use tiles glazed in golden yellow. In Beijing, all buildings must be lower than the main halls in the Forbidden City. In short, the monarchical power was absolute, and brooked no infringement.

Temples and Altars

Ancient Chinese attached great importance to rituals dedicated to the Heaven, the Earth, the ancestor and the supernatural. Far back in

The Altar of the Land and Grain, Beijing.

the Zhou period about 2,500 years ago, these rituals were already institutionalized and became a part of the hierarchical system. Because of this, imperial temples and altars always had the highest status and, therefore, were the most imposing and magnificent of their kind found anywhere in the country. As we see from those preserved to this day in Beijing, there were stringent rules governing the location of each imperial temple or shrine. The Temple of Heaven lies to the south of the Forbidden City; the Temple of Earth, to the north; the Temple of the Sun, to the east, and the Temple of the Moon, to the west. The Imperial Ancestral Temple and the Altar to the Gods of the Earth and Grains are in the center of the capital city, to the upper left and upper right of the Forbidden City, respectively. The way imperial temples and altars are arranged is culturally significant, indeed.

Ancient China was predominantly an agricultural country. For this reason, what is known as *"she ji"* (earth and grains) was the symbol of the nation. Far back in remote antiquity, the Chinese were already worshipping the gods of the earth and grains. What is now the Zhongshan Park to the right of the Gate of Heavenly Peace, the main gate of the Forbidden City, is the site of the Altar to the Gods of the Earth and Grains in the Ming and Qing dynasties. The altar is an earthen platform about one meter high, with each side about 15 meters long. Its surface is covered with earth of five colors. A strip of yellow earth is in the middle of the altar, which is surrounded by strips of earth red, white, black and greenish black in color that face south, west, north and east separately. While denoting the five azimuths of China's territory, the altar embodies the notion summarized as "every inch of land in the country is a part of the monarchical domain". The Imperial Ancestral Temple, which is now the Cultural Palace of the Laboring People, lies to the left of the Gate of Heavenly Peace. In both the Ming and Qing dynasties, sacrificial ceremonies were held on most important festival occasions in honor of the imperial families' ancestors. The temple is a neat cluster of buildings in three courtyards separated by walls. The Frontal

Hall of Prayer for Good Harvest in the Heavenly Temple, Beijing. The round roof of the structure and the walled courtyard in the shape of a neat square enliven the traditional belief that the Heaven is round and the land is a neat square. Note the roofs of the structures. These are blue in color, the color of the Heaven as ancient Chinese thought it to be.

Hall, Middle Hall and Rear Hall are the main structures and on either side of them there is a row of side halls.

Elaborate sacrificial ceremonies were held every year in all Chinese dynasties, at which emperors begged the gods of the sun, moon, heaven and earth for good weather, bumper harvests and peace and prosperity of the country and people. The ceremony in honor of the Heaven was the most important, as emperors, those self-styled *"tian zi"* (son of the Heaven), claimed to rule the country and people on His behalf. To hold Heaven-worshipping ceremonies was the emperors' exclusive privilege, and anybody else would risk having his or her head cut off for even attempting to hold one. The Temple of Heaven in Beijing is the largest and the best preserved of its kind in China - in fact it occupies an area three times as large as the

Memorial temple dedicated to the ancestors of all those in Guangdong whose family name is Chen. The perfectly preserved structure was built more than 100 years ago.

Forbidden City[1]. The Circular Mound Altar, the Imperial Vault of Heaven and the Hall of Prayer for Good Harvests, which are built in a straight line from south to north, are the main structures in the Temple of Heaven. The Circular Mound Altar, a triple-tiered white stone terrace surrounded by white marble balustrades, was the site for ceremonies in honor of the Heaven. The Imperial Vault of Heaven is a round, single-story structure where the tablet in honor of the Heaven was placed. In front of the entrance of the structure lies a round enclosure surrounded by a thick wall of polished bricks. One highly popular attraction here is the Echo Wall, which was so cleverly built that a mere whisper close to it can be clearly heard at any other point on the wall. To the north of the Imperial Vault of Heaven lies the Hall of Prayer for Good Harvests, a lofty cone-shaped structure with triple eaves. As its name suggests, the structure, in itself, is a symbol of China's agricultural culture. There are four main columns in the hall, which symbolize the four seasons of the year. Twelve pillars support the first or the lowest eave, symbolizing the 12 two-hour periods into which the day was traditionally divided. Pillars of the same number support the eave in the middle, symbolizing the 12 months of the year. The 24 pillars represent the 24 divisions of the year by China's traditional lunar calendar.

Ancient Chinese were deeply family-bound. More often than not, people of the same family line living in the same village or the same villages in a given area formed a clan-based autonomous body. The head of a clan, normally a male elder who commanded high respect of the clan, supervised over the handling of important affairs related to the clan. This autonomous body was well organized, preserved by a set of patriarchal rules and regulations that observed a stringent order of the senior and the junior, those born of legal wives and those born of concubines, and those who were masters and those who were servants. This patriarchal system was, in fact, the foundation of China's feudal government, an instrument by means of which government decisions on political and public affairs were executed. The clan saw to it that the different families pay taxes in time. It was also responsible for mediating settlement of disputes, "enlightening" clan members through education, and organizing sacrificial activities in honor of gods and ancestors. Each clan had an ancestral hall or temple. While the venue of sacrificial activities, the ancestral hall or temple was the clan's meeting place or the clan's courtroom where disputes were settled and those having broken clan rules punished. Many ancestral temples had theaters, schools and public granary where relief grain was stored. Ancestral temples were often larger in size and better in construction quality than residential buildings of the average level. The more powerful and prosperous a clan was, the larger and more magnificent would be its ancestral temple. The temple, as a matter of fact, was the symbol of the past glory of the clan and its present prosperity and influence. As such, it normally consisted of several courtyards with richly decorated halls.

Residential Buildings

In China, residential buildings are diverse in style and structure

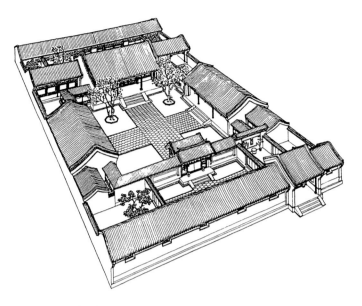

Diagrammatic sketch of a typical *si he yuan* (traditional courtyard) in Beijing.

as natural conditions and folkways differ from place to place.

In north China, *si he yuan* are the most popular housing buildings in traditional style. A *si he yuan* is a rectangular compound with traditional one-story houses of gray tiles and bricks built on the four sides of it. The compound would have been totally enclosed but for the gate, while doors and windows of the houses invariably open to the inside. A standard *si he yuan* compound consists of two yards, the fore-yard and the backyard. Rooms in the south of the fore yard are used as guest rooms or studies. The backyard is the family's living quarters. Patriarchal rules are strictly observed in distributing the rooms among members of the family. The main rooms, which face south and are the largest and brightest, are reserved for the seniors, while the juniors live in rooms of the east and west rows. The main rooms are fitted with side rooms, which are used as kitchens, toilets or storerooms. A large *si he yuan* compound may have four or even five courtyards, often with a private garden in the backyard.

By tradition, nomads in China's far north live in yurts. But along with economic development and social progress increasing numbers of them have come to settle in one-story buildings of earth and timber. Cave dwellings constitute a unique scene in the cold, dry loess highlands of northwest China, where the earthen slopes are solid enough to be dug in. There are also "underground cave dwellings" or "underground compounds". In constructing this kind of cave dwellings, people dig a deep well on a piece of flatland, and then dig into the walls of the well for space to live in while planting flowers in the bottom of the well. "Barking of dogs can be heard but no human being can be seen" - this old saying is a vivid description of those underground cave dwellings or underground compounds. No matter where they are dug, on slopes or on walls of wells, cave dwellings are cost effective in construction while able to afford sufficient comfort all the year round. It is, in fact, cool in summer and warm in winter inside of cave dwellings.

In south China, walled compounds and clusters of residential buildings without courtyards can both be found. Southern Anhui and northern Jiangxi are known for *tian jing* - "heavenly wells" — that are actually small yards. The yard is the center of a "heavenly well", with multi-story buildings built on all or the rear, left and right sides

A cone-shaped *tu lou* compound in Fujian Province.

Farm houses in Jiangxi Province.

of it to prevent the scorching sun from slanting into the compound directly and allow sufficient ventilation the same way as a chimney. The yard receives water discharged from the rooms. This practice, known locally as "rivers from the four directions collecting in the yard", may be related to the old tradition summarized as "letting no rich water flow into other families' fields". Moreover, the yard is often fitted with exterior fireproof walls. These walls, which are high enough to overlook the buildings in the yard, are whitewashed while the top is built of bluish black tiles, thus forming a pleasant contrast.

Of residential buildings of all types found anywhere in China - maybe anywhere in the world, *tu lou* compounds popular in parts of Fujian and southern Jiangxi are probably the most unique in construction style and structure. Seen from a distance, *tu lou* compounds, cone-shaped or rectangular, look like castles. A *tu lou* compound is enclosed by a round wall of rammed earth up to two meters thick and as tall as a four- or five-story building, with a few window-like holes dug through its upper part. A cone-shaped *tu lou* compound of the average size is somewhere between 50 and 60 meters in diameters, but there are larger ones with a diameter as great as 90 meters. Buildings inside the compound form three circles with the smallest in the center. Buildings of four or five stories form the outer circle. Kitchens and storerooms are on the first floor, rooms on the second floor are used as granaries, and residential quarters are on the third and higher floors. The circle in the middle is the ancestral hall, which is also the venue of clan meetings, weddings and memorial services. A *tu lou* compound is home to scores of families belonging to the same clan. This phenomenon, which is not to be found elsewhere in the world, is attributed to wars in ancient times that forced people in the north to flee to Fujian, Guangdong and other parts of China's deep south. The immigrants, known as "Hakkas" or "guest people", were not to live in peace, as clashes with natives were common occurrences due to cultural and psychological differences and conflicting interests. In order to survive, families of a Hakka clan had to live together and, as time went by, learned to build those castle-like *tu lou* compounds for self-defense. But thanks to this, ancient clan culture and folkways have been preserved to this day.

In China's deep south, people of ethnic minority groups live mainly in rainy, hot mountainous areas. For ventilation and protection from animals and insects, they prefer to live in houses on raised platforms built with locally available materials. The Dais in Yunnan Province lives in areas where bamboo groves thrive, hence their bamboo huts built on platforms of bamboo tilts. Bedrooms and guestrooms are in the upper part of the structure, while the lower part - the part below the platform - is used as animal sheds or storerooms.

Classical Gardens

The earliest gardens came into being in the 11th century BC as pleasure grounds for aristocrats. These were, in fact, natural sites enclosed for hunting or animal farms with facilities for wining and dining. As time went by, people began building gardens. Most gardens in classical style we are still able to visit were built in the Ming-Qing period, the period that represented the highest achievements in traditional Chinese architectural art.

Imperial gardens were mostly built in the capital city and its surrounding areas. Virtually all the imperial gardens were built in areas north of the Yangtze River, the center of political activities in feudal China. Imperial gardens were invariably large. They were beautiful with not only natural landscapes but also with man-made scenic spots like towers and pavilions. Many Chinese emperors spent their lives in their gardens, handling court affairs while enjoying themselves in luxury and splendor. Yuan Ming Yuan, or the Garden of Perfect Splendor on the western outskirts of Beijing, is recognized as the largest imperial garden ever built in ancient China. Construction of the garden began in 1701, the 40th year of the reign of Emperor Kang Xi of the Qing Dynasty. Succeeding emperors continued building and expanding the garden - the "garden of all gardens" as it was known in the West — until an Anglo-French army set it ablaze in the Second Opium War of 1860.[2] The largest imperial garden preserved to this day is Yi He Yuan, the Garden of Perfect Harmony

Doors of a structure in a classical-style garden may well be compared to the viewfinder of a camera. Here is an example taken from the Slender West Lake, a scenic spot in Yangzhou City, Jiangsu Province.

Buddha Worshipping Pavilion atop the hill that overlooks Lake Kunming, the landmark of the Summer Palace.

or the Summer Palace, which is also on the outskirts of Beijing.

Private gardens of classical style are found mainly in areas south of the Yangtze River, particular in Suzhou and Yangzhou of Jiangsu Province and Hangzhou of Zhejiang. Most of these were built and owned by rich merchants and ranking officials, who often doubled as scholars. Private gardens, such as those preserved to this day, are relatively small. Though limited in space, these invariably feature a perfect harmony of natural and artificial beauty with streams, pavilions, corridors, flowers, exotic rocks and pools that were meant to create an environment of peace, tranquility and urbanity for study and scholarly encounter. Gardens in Suzhou are regarded as the best examples of classical Chinese gardening.

China also boasts a wide range of "open gardens" — natural scenic

Wanshi Garden in Suzhou, Jiangsu Province. This private
garden was built in the Qing Dynasty (1644-1911).

spots near cities, towns and other population centers where there are
classical style buildings like Buddhist and Taoist temples. Rules of
traditional gardening were followed even though no one had ever
planned the development of the sites. "Open gardens" feature a
combination of natural beauty with folk culture, sites of historic
interest and landscape of humanities related to folkways and legends.
The picturesque West Lake in Hangzhou is the most famous "open
garden" in China.

In China, temples and other religious shrines are often found in
forests and mountains far away from population centers as Buddhists
and Taoists like to engage in worshipping and practice austerities in
seclusion and tranquility. Temples are often known for the mountains
where they are. Likewise, mountains are famous because of the
temples in them. But temples in densely populated cities and towns
are also ideal for religious practices, and these are constructed and

greened in such a way as to allow sufficient seclusion and tranquility. In fact such temples are, in themselves, gardens. To name just two of the best known "temple gardens" - Tan Tuo Si (Temple of the Pool and White Mulberry) in Beijing and Ling Yin Si (Temple of Inspired Seclusion) in Hangzhou.

Pursuit of natural beauty - natural beauty even in what is artificial - is the most salient feature of traditional Chinese gardening. Everything in a classical Chinese garden - a bridge, a pavilion, a corridor or even a rock - is arranged in such a way as to make one feel as if in a natural surrounding. In artistic style, traditional Chinese gardens are definitely different from gardens in the West where one may take in everything at a glance - those structures always in symmetrical order, those lawns invariably large, and those plants cut and pruned in a way that form geometric patterns.

1. The Temple of Heaven is 270 hectares large, compared with the Forbidden City that occupies an area of 72 hectares.

2. When in its full grandeur, the Garden of Perfect Splendor had more than 140 scenic spots featuring not only traditional Chinese structures but also structures of Western styles. It occupied an area of 370 hectares, and the wall round the garden was 10 kilometers long.

Confucianism - the Most Essential Part of the Traditional Chinese Culture

A Hundred Contending Schools of Thought

During the Spring and Autumn and the Warring States periods, persistent social upheavals and incessant wars gave rise to what historians call "a hundred contending schools of thought". The number "a hundred" shouldn't be understood literally. It refers to a situation in which there were numerous philosophies and schools of thoughts. The most important schools of thought, however, were Confucianism (*ru jia*), Mohism *(mo jia)*, Taoism *(dao jia)*[1] and Legalism *(fa jia)*. Though different in philosophical approaches or ways of looking at society, these four greatest schools of thought were all concerned with the question of how to organize society to ensure happiness of the population and prosperity of the country.

Mohism and Confucianism had the greatest number of followers and were the most influential during the Spring and Autumn and Warring States periods. And for this reason, they were called *xian xue* - meaning the "prominent philosophies". The founder of Mohism was Mo Zi (468-376 BC). He attributed social upheavals to failure on the part of the people to love each other. Basing himself on this understanding, Mo Zi stood for universal love and was strongly opposed to wars. His ideas are found in a book entitled *Mo Zi*. The book also contains the philosopher's teachings on the need to practice frugality on funerals and other important occasions and to oppose unnecessary and over-elaborate formalities in social life. Besides, the philosopher called for selecting the right persons to govern and stood against inherited property and aristocratic titles. Though he thought that religious beliefs were necessary, he attached much importance to studies of the worldly life and practical problems in society. He took light of the family, and he was in fact opposed to division of society by family lines. To sum up, the theories of Mohism ran diametrically in counter to the patriarchal tradition characteristic of the Chinese society. And simply for this reason, the philosophy of Mohism would not be acceptable to any of the feudal dynasties after his times.

Lao Zi, roughly a contemporary of Confucius (551-479 BC) of the Spring and Autumn period, was the founder of the philosophy known as Taoism. The book *Lao Zi*, which has been attributed to him, was actually a work of the Warring States period that followed the Spring and Autumn period. Zhuang Zi (369-286 BC) inherited Taoism and developed it. Exponents of Taoism were opposed to oppressive government and stood for what is known as "government by non-interference" - government by allowing matters to take their own course of development. According to Taoist doctrines, an ideal society should have a small population and territory. In such a society, people lived a simple life, were free from any material pursuit and

The mural, found in Qinglong Temple of Shanxi Province, depicts men and women of great virtue.

would never visit people of neighboring states even though "they could hear the crowing of cocks and the barking of dogs on the other side of the border". The philosophy held social progress in contempt, and called for return of society to its original simplicity, to the time when people recorded events by making knots on a rope. In later years, Taoism became a supplement to Confucianism, the dominating ideology in feudal China. As such, it was able to exert a sustaining influence on the Chinese people in their outlook of the world. People in literati and officialdom were invariably inspired by its call for return to nature, and that explains why many of them would withdraw from society and live in seclusion when they failed to realize their political ideals or ambitions.

Han Fei (280-233 BC) was the most outstanding exponent of Legalism which, unlike Confucianism that called for government by benevolence and rites that supposedly governed the behavior of the nobles beginning as of the West Zhou period, stood for stronger monarchical rule and government by law. Legalists held that a sovereign did not have to be exceptionally talented or moral conscious, and that his only job was to make laws and decrees known to his subjects. Moreover, laws and decrees must be severe and justice must be administered inflexibly in following the principle of all people being equal before law irrespective of their social status. In other words, the sovereign should mete out rewards and punishments indiscriminately. Exponents of Legalism held that law enforcement was meant to ensure implementation of any order from the sovereign. They also believed that there should a complete set of methods and skills - political artifices, as a matter of fact — for choosing the right kind of people to do the right kind of jobs and to handle affairs of government. Only in this way, they argued, would it be possible for the sovereign not to become a mere figurehead. Legalist ideas were

▶ *Six Men of Virtue in a Bamboo Grove at the Side of a Stream.* The painting enlivens the Taoist way of life that calls for harmony between Man and nature and freedom from vulgarity.

to exert a strong influence on politics in feudal China. Basing himself on these ideas, Emperor Shi Huang of the Qin Dynasty established China's first centralized feudal monarchy after he unified China in 221 BC.

Confucius

Confucius (551-479 BC), whose family name was Kong and his given name, Qiu, hailed from the State of Lu in the Spring and Autumn period. He was born in what is now Qufu city in Shandong Province, east China.

While a great thinker, educator and scholar, Confucius was a keen, tireless learner. One of his most quoted sayings goes like this: If three of us walk together, at least one of the other two is good enough to be my teacher. During his youth, Confucius was for a time a petty official managing government warehouses; and then he tended cattle and sheep for the government. For the most part of his life, however, he was a private tutor. He often toured other states to promote his political ideas, taking with him some of his students. The rulers of these states all received him courteously and consulted him, but never did he have an opportunity to put into practice his theory of government. Not until his 50s did he become an official in charge of criminal punishment and maintenance of social order in the State of Lu. On that post he was able to participate in state administration, but before long he resigned on discovery that his political ideas differed from those of the sovereign. He devoted his later years to collation and editing of literary works. He was said to have edited the *Book of History* and the *Book of Odes*. He added explanatory notes to the *Book of Changes*. He compiled the *Spring and Autumn Annals,* and examined and revised the *Book of Rites* and the *Book of Music.* The *Book of Odes* is the earliest collection of Chinese folk songs. While a book of divination popular in the Zhou period, the *Book of Changes* has been taken as a treasure house of political wisdom and ways of handling things. The *Spring and Autumn Annals* was a chronicle of events that took place in the State of Lu. The

Parts of a Ming Dynasty (1368-1644) scroll depicting life and work of the Chinese sage Confucius – travelling between different states to promote his ideas, teaching, etc.

Book of History is a collection of documents of the Xia, Shang and Zhou periods. In the *Book of Rites,* Confucius recorded those elaborate rites and protocols dating to the Zhou period. These books were to be called the "six classics of Confucianism" even though the *Book of Music* has been lost. After Confucius died, his disciples compiled his statements and ideas to form a book entitled the *Analects of Confucius* which, like the "six classics", must be studied and followed in real earnest by all scholars in feudal China.

Confucius established a complete system of ethics centered on

ren - meaning "virtue" or "benevolence". He believed that the "benevolent loves others". In other words, Confucius held that people should love each other. But what one should do to put the principle into practice? First of all, he insisted, one must constantly improve oneself to be perfect in virtue. On this question, he had this to say: "One must improve oneself in order to improve others; and one must enlighten oneself in order to enlighten others." Secondly, he held that one must consider others in one's own place. "Do not do to others what you do not want to be done to yourself," he said. Confucius was the staunchest exponent of *li*. The Chinese character *li* literally means "courtesy", "etiquette", "protocol", etc. But in a broader sense it means the "code of social conduct". By advocating *li,* Confucius meant to educate the masses of people in the importance of following the ancient rites and observing the established rules governing social conduct, so that each would acquire a perfect understanding of his or her place in the family and society. Order and harmony of the family and society would be maintained only when due attention was paid to precedence dividing the senior and the junior and the ruler and the ruled. Confucius attached much importance to virtue while taking light of self-interest, always stressing the importance of self-cultivation on the part of the individual to the maintenance of social order and government of the state. He stood for benevolent rule by the sovereign and called for an economic policy that was effective enough to ensure tangible benefits to the people. On politics, he advocated leniency in meting out punishments while stressing the need to maintain order through enlightenment and education of the population.

Before Confucius initiated private teaching, education had been provided only at government-run schools and limited to children of the nobility. Confucius was the first to have broken this monopoly. His own principle called for providing "proper education to people of all status". It is said that he had more than 3,000 students, 70 of whom won public recognition as *xian ren* - "persons of virtue".

Confucianism in Later Years

After Confucius died, there emerged different schools of the philosophy he founded. Of these, the most influential were those founded by Mencius (active between 372 BC and 289 BC) and Xun Zi (active during 298-238 BC). Mencius inherited the Confucian concept of virtue and rule by benevolence, believing that man was born with goodness. He stood for the "kingly way" of government while condemning tyranny, and urged sovereigns of his times to rule by benevolence the same way as ancient sages and men of virtue had. He made the point that "people are the most important, followed by the land and grain while the sovereign comes last in importance". In the Han Dynasty, the Mencius doctrine came to be recognized as the orthodox of Confucianism. In the Song Dynasty, the *Analects of Mencius*, a collection of statements by Mencius, was made a classical work of Confucianism like the *Analects of Confucius*.

Xun Zi was against fatalism and superstitious beliefs in supernaturals. He believed that man was born vicious. He developed the Confucian idea of government by using the system of precedence dividing the senior from the junior and the ruler from the ruled, and

Shu yuan, or "academies of learning", was where scholars gathered to study, assemble collections of books, confer on scholarly issues and teach. Picture shows Yue Lu Academy of Learning in Changsha City, Hunan Province, which was started in the year 976.

called for still more stringent rules to specify the social status of each. In politics, Xun Zi stood for combining rule by rites and rule by law, that is, for using the "kingly way" and tyranny alternately to administer the country. Because of this, his ideas came to be incorporated into theories of Legalism. It may be interesting to note that Han Fei Zi, the chief exponent of Legalism, and Li Si, a Legalist who served as Emperor Shi Huang's prime minister, were Xun Zi's students.

During the Spring and Autumn and Warring States periods, none of the sovereigns paid much attention to Confucianism even though it was a "prominent school of thought" like Taoism and Legalism. In the Han Dynasty, however, a historic change took place in the status of Confucianism. On proposal of Dong Zhongshu (179-104 BC), a most prominent scholar of Confucianism, Emperor Wu Di, who ruled China from 139 BC to 87 BC, adopted Confucianism as the official philosophy and denied scholars of all other schools of the opportunity to enter civil service. Yet it must be noted that by the time the policy of "making Confucianism supreme while letting all other schools pass into oblivion" was adopted, Confucianism had already become different from what it used to be. To put it in another way, it had become something that combined the Confucian idea of rule by benevolence with the Legalist idea of rule by law, something that had also drawn on theories of other schools. As Confucian dogmatists of the Han and succeeding dynasties bitterly put it, Confucianism of the Han Dynasty was "Confucianism only in appearance but Legalist in essence". To be more precise, the Confucian aspect of this combination influenced the country's social organization, ethics and moral standards, ideology and culture, and the Legalist aspect manifested itself mainly in feudal China's political theories and practices.

While inheriting the doctrines of Confucius and Mencius, Confucianism of the Song Dynasty, or "neo-Confucianism" as it is known in the West, featured numerous ideas borrowed from Buddhism and Taoism. Its theory centered on cultivation of one's

In ancient China, stone arches were often built in honor of people of great virtue – loyal officials and soldiers, filial children, widows who refused to remarry, etc. This arch in in Shexian County, Anhui Province, is dedicated to Xu Guo, an upright official of the Ming Dynasty.

inner world in relation to society and politics. It stressed the vital need for individuals to abide by the code of conduct and moral obligations prevalent in feudal China. To be precise, it demanded absolute allegiance to those "cardinal guides and constant virtues" in the feudal ethical code - loyalty, filial piety, chastity and righteousness. It urged people to pay the utmost attention to moral integrity, and went so far as to demand that individuals be absolutely free from human desires.

For well over 2,000 years beginning as of the Han Dynasty, Confucianism was the dominating ideology in monarchical China. Memorial temples in honor of Confucius the Sage were built in all cities and towns, where elaborate rituals were held by emperors and officials every year to offer sacrifices in his honor. As a matter of fact, monarchs of each feudal dynasty would try their best to prove that they were more faithful to Confucianism and cared more of the

Sage than previous monarchs. Confucius, who accomplished almost nothing in politics when alive, would have never dreamed that he was to be lauded to the skies centuries after he died. The craze went on until after the 1911 Revolution that toppled the Qing, China's last feudal dynasty, and ushered in an intellectual campaign to criticize Confucianism.

Education in Ancient China

Schools in ancient China fell into two categories, "official schools" run either by the central or the local governments and private schools. Imperial schools were called *tai xue* (the "supreme school") or *guo zi jian* (directorate of learning). Emperor Wu Di of the Han Dynasty set up ancient China's first *tai xue* to "cultivate talents and prepare them for officialdom". The Han Dynasty's *tai xue* had more than 30,000 students at the height of its development in the early second century. In most cases, a later dynasty named the highest imperial school either *tai xue* or *guo zi jian*. When a dynasty had both, *guo zi jian* was meant for children of the most senior members of the ruling

Boisterous Children and the Sleeping Teacher,
a Qing Dynasty (1644-1911) painting.

A private school in Qing Dynasty (1644-1911).

class. In all cases, classics of Confucianism were the main subjects on the curriculum, though the *tai xue* or *guo zi jian* of some dynasties had faculties of military art, mathematics, medicine, painting, etc.

"Official schools" had a limited enrolment and the vast majority of the ancient Chinese had to rely on private schools for education. Private schools, which were initiated by Confucius, played a predominant role in education in all dynasties.

Non-Confucian schools of thought had no place in official schools. Like official schools, private schools, in general, took classics of Confucianism as the main subject. But there were private schools that taught non-Confucian philosophies. Only because of this, non-Confucian philosophies were able to survive the official discrimination and be passed down from one generation of Chinese scholars to the next.

Private schools were divided into several types. There were those run by individuals who made a living by teaching. Besides, there were family schools run by rich merchants, landlords and officials for education of their own children and children of their close relatives or friends. Some private schools were funded by private donations or rental receipts from land belonging to ancestral or religious temples, and therefore did not charge students of tuition. Private schools were, in fact, the only institutions of primary education for the vast majority of ancient Chinese. In a private school, children began by learning to read and write the characters. After learning enough characters by heart, they would be taught classics of Confucianism and composition, as well writing of classical essays and poetry.

Shu yuan, or "academies of learning" where scholars gathered to study, assemble collections of books, confer on scholarly issues and teach, also played an important role in education and academic research in ancient China. These were invariably started or supervised by prestigious scholars. The earliest *shu yuan* came into being in the Tang Dynasty. In Song Dynasty such establishments thrived, mostly at scenic spots or places of historic interest far away from population centers. Large numbers of scholars gathered there for study of Confucian classics and discussion of current affairs. The Yuan Dynasty that succeeded the Song tightened control over *shu yuan*, and so did the next dynasty, the Ming. In the Qing Dynasty, *shu yuan* were operating as quasi-official establishments where scholars sought advanced studies in preparation for participation in imperial examinations.

The Imperial Examination System

Confucius had this to say: "Officialdom is the natural course of development for good scholars." The Sage's teaching inspired countless ancient Chinese scholars with an ambition to become a part of the ruling elite through study. The system of imperial civil service examinations, which was practiced for well over 1,300 years, was the institutional guarantee for realization of this ambition.

In the Han Dynasty, the central government sent out officials to different places to directly select from among young scholars those few for admission into *tai xue,* where classics of Confucianism were taught. Young scholars who excelled in study and virtue may also attend the "supreme school" on recommendation of local

Guo Zi Jian in Beijing was the imperial university or the highest directorate of learning under three successive dynasties, the Yuan, Ming and Qing. Picture shows the gate of its inner courtyard.

governments. If a *tai xue* student wanted to become an official, he must work hard on Confucian classics in the school in order to pass the imperial civil service examination. So the Han Dynasty initiated the education system based on Confucianism and the system of selecting officials through examination. But it was up to the nobility and high ministers to decide whom to be chosen as candidates for officialdom and, more often than not, people who were genuinely talented were rejected. As time went by, the power fell into the hands of powerful, influential families of aristocracy and family status became the sole criterion. As a result, the ruling elite came to consist purely of those from upper class families.

In the Sui Dynasty, the imperial civil service examination system changed, in such a way as to oblige any one wanting to become an official to pass examinations at different levels, from lower to higher, from local to central, irrespective of his family background. These examinations were sponsored by the government, and took place simultaneously across the country. This way of selecting officials through competitive examinations and without regard to family status imbued scholars with hope and gave them an opportunity, in that it became possible for even a peasant boy to become somebody if only he studied hard enough. Meanwhile, it gave rise to the belief that "all occupations are low, and only book-learning is exalted." When granting an audience to winners of a top-level imperial examination, Li Shimin, the second emperor of the Tang Dynasty, was so pleased that he couldn't refrain from exclaiming: "All heroes in the country are in my hands."

While classics of Confucianism was the main subject, candidates in imperial examinations had been tested in mathematics, law, political science and current affairs. But step by step, Confucian orthodox and essay writing based on that became the only subjects. The final result was that though theoretically open to everybody, officialdom came to be meant largely for those with enough time and money to prepare themselves for imperial examinations. In other words, the ruling elite came to consist mainly of the intellectual elite.

As Confucian classics were the main subject of civil service examinations, these, as a matter of course, were the textbooks for schools of all

Imperial examination as depicted in a Yuan Dynasty (1271-1368) painting.

Sacrificial ceremony in honor of Confucius at the
Confucius Mansion in Qufu, Shandong Province.

types and at all levels. Scholars of all dynasties made annotations to
Confucian classics, and the government would designate annotated
versions up to the best standard for use as official textbooks. This
meant that to be successful in imperial examinations, one would have
no other way out but to follow official annotations when elaborating
on doctrines of Confucianism. Under so rigid a control by the
government, any school of thought would eventually become
stereotyped. This state of affairs was driven to the extreme in the
Ming and Qing dynasties. On order of the government, word-by-
word quotes from the *Analects of Confucius* were used as topics for
examinations, and participants in examinations were not allowed to
express their personal views when elaborating. The literary
compositions prescribed for examinations, known as the "eight-part
essays", were in fact infamous for rigidity in form and poverty of
ideas. Students preparing themselves for examinations had to learn
by rote, paying no attention to knowledge and skills of practical use.
Development of natural sciences was ignored as a result, because
one's knowledge of natural sciences was not tested in examinations.
The last imperial civil service examination was held in 1905, and six

years afterwards, the Qing, China's last feudal dynasty, was toppled.

The Cultural Sphere of Confucianism

Korea, Vietnam and Japan, together with China, form a cultural sphere of Confucianism. Doctrines of the Chinese sage have been able to exert a far-reaching influence on all aspects of social life in these countries - social, political, educational and academic.

In the third century BC, Confucian doctrines, along with Chinese characters, found their way into the Korean Peninsula, and in later centuries became the dominating ideology of the states there. State institutions of learning modeled after those of the Tang Dynasty China were set up, and officials came to be selected through competitive examinations in Confucianism the same way as in China. While sending students to China, the various states on the peninsula made teaching of Confucianism compulsory at schools. Korean sovereigns attached much importance to filial piety, commending those who were filial and punishing those who were not. Ancient Korean children were taught to be filial to their elders and asked to translate filial piety into loyalty to the sovereign when they grew up.

In the third century, there emerged in Japan schools teaching

A Confucius Temple in Japan. It was built in 1893.

Confucian classics to princes and high ministers. The sixth century Japan saw a massive invasion of Chinese culture, when returned scholars, diplomatic envoys, monks and handicraftsmen brought back not only skills and knowledge but also ideas. The Japanese borrowed from Chinese characters in forming their own written language, and spared no effort to promote education in Confucianism. While continuing to develop the indigenous religion called Shindo, they accepted the kind of Buddhism that had already become a part of the Chinese culture. After the Taika reform of the 7th century, a centralized monarchy modeled after China under the Tang Dynasty was established in Japan. Even today, influence of the traditional Chinese culture remains evident, as shown in written Japanese

As an ideological system, Confucianism has become outdated along with the rise of capitalism and modern thoughts of democracy and science. But some of the thinking models and ethnical standards characteristic of Confucianism may transcend times. These include benevolence and virtue, respect for the elder and love of the young, subordinating interests of the individual to the interests of the collective, devotion to the public and state interests without thought of self, and being the first to bear hardships and the last to enjoy comfort. For China of today, there is the vital need to promote these moral standards while carrying forward the spirit of hard work and diligence in striving for modernization. And precisely because of this, attempts are being made in light of modernity to interpret Confucianism - a most essential part of the traditional Chinese culture.

1. Taoism was a most influential philosophical school in the Spring and Autumn period. But in later centuries it was taken as the philosophical basis of the indigenous Chinese religion also called "Taoism".

Literature and Art - the Spirit of the Chinese Nation

Chinese Literature

Poetry was the earliest and also the best developed literary form in ancient China. The *Book of Odes* is the earliest collection of Chinese poetry, which has 305 poems that date to the period from the 11th century to the 6th century BC. Of these, the best are *guo feng* or *feng* - folk songs collected from 15 dukedoms of the Zhou period. In later years, *Chu ci,* another form of poetry, was developed on the basis of folk songs in areas south on the middle and lower reaches of the Yangtze River — the "Chu" region. Along with the rise of *Chu ci* came the *Songs of the South*, the second earliest collection of Chinese poetry after the *Book of Odes*. Qu Yuan (about 340-278 BC) was the most outstanding representative of the *Chu ci* school of Chinese poetry, and his best known work is *Li Sao*, which means "lamentation". *Guo feng*, or *feng,* initiated China's literary tradition of realism, and *Li Sao*, also known as *Sao*, ushered in the style of romanticism in Chinese literature, hence the formulation *feng Sao* (literary excellence).

The Tang Dynasty was the golden age for Chinese poetry. Poetry writing and recitation were a fashion everywhere, from imperial palaces and residences of ranking officials to singsong houses and even brothels. So long as he was good at poetry, a candidate for the imperial examination could still pass even if he failed in the test in Confucian classics. Numerous poets made a name for themselves in the history of Chinese literature, and even today, Tang poems are still read and studied as best examples of classical Chinese poetry. The *Complete Collection of Tang Poems,* which was compiled in the 18th century on order of Emperor Kang Xi of the Qing Dynasty, has 49,403 poems by 2,837 poets. Li Bai (701-762), the "god of poetry", and Du Fu (712-

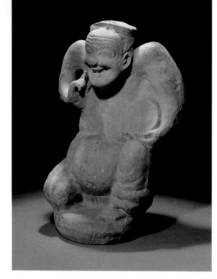

A Han Dynasty (206 BC-220 AD) "ballad singer".

770), the "sage of poetry", represented the highest achievements in Tang poetry. Li's poems are reputed for an unrestrained, flowing grace. In comparison, Du's poems feature profound pathos that stemmed from his concern with the destiny of the country and sufferings of the people. It may well be said that their works are classical examples of literary romanticism and realism, respectively.

Ci poems of the Song Dynasty are equally important in the history of Chinese literature. Unlike Tang poems written by an intellectual elite, *ci* poetry originated from folksongs and ballads popular in urban centers, and thanks to polishing by the literati of the late Tang period, these eventually became an independent literary form. A large number of outstanding *ci* poets came to the fore in the Song Dynasty. Among them, Su Shi (1037-1101) and Xin Qiji (1140-1207) were the highest representatives of the powerful and free school of *ci* writing, as opposed to Li Qingzhao (F., 1084-about 1151) and Liu Yong (?-about 1053) who were rated as the greatest *ci* poets of the subtle and concise school. Chinese poetry is so beautiful and elegant, leading to the popular belief that recitation of good poems helps improve one's quality. Today, as in the past, rarely one finds an intellectual who cannot recite a few Tang poems or Song *ci*.

Metaphor was the rhetoric technique most frequently used in composing classical Chinese poems. That may help explain why unlike Western poetry, classical Chinese poetry tends to be restrained in expressing the feelings of the poets. "Words few but feelings profound and boundless" - this is a most important criterion for judging the quality of a poem - nay, of art works in all its forms including traditional paintings. In some cases, a poet made a point by implying his or her

Cui Yingying, the heroine of the *West Chamber*, is reading a letter from her secret lover.

real meaning instead of making it explicit. This, plus the fact that classical Chinese is extremely terse, makes it almost impossible for translations of classical Chinese poetry to retain the original style and flavor.

Relative to lyrics, narrative literature came late and was not as developed. This is, in part, because the country does not have an epic of global importance like Odyssey.[4] By tradition, poetry and prose were seen as the orthodox of literature while fictions and drama, as relatively low in artistic taste and intellectual quality. It was not until the period spanning from the 14th century to the 18th did fiction and drama writing become able to thrive. Despite so strong a social discrimination, writers of the Ming and Qing Dynasties produced a host of novels that have been popular ever since they came into being. Of these, four are recognized as the greatest: *Romance of the Three Kingdoms* by Luo Guanzhong (about 1330-about 1400); *Water Margin* by Shi Nai'an, a writer of late Yuan or early Ming period; *Pilgrimage to the West* by Wu Cheng'en (about 1500-about 1580); and *A Dream of Red Mansions* by Cao Xueqin (about 1715-1764). *A Dream of Red Mansions,* in particular, has been acclaimed as the pinnacle of China's novel writing. By recounting the tragic love between the hero and heroine and the rise and fall of an aristocratic family, it unfolds a panorama of China's feudal society and the way of the world in it. The novel was an instant hit. So went the saying, "All books come to nothing now that there is *A Dream of Red Mansions*."

Generally speaking, politics and ethics are the dominating themes of classical Chinese literary works, a phenomenon largely attributed to the traditional concept that regards poetry and prose as meant for enlightening the people. Meanwhile, poets and painters were strongly influenced by the Taoist philosophy that calls for spiritual freedom and idealizes the nature. That explains why nature was also a most important theme for classical Chinese literary and art works.

Traditional Chinese Paintings

Traditional Chinese paintings constitute a unique school of fine art, a school that, in style and techniques, is vastly different from any other fine art school in the world. Traditional Japanese fine art may be the only exception, but it has to be remembered that it has been heavily influenced by the Chinese culture.

The Chinese do paintings with brushes. Dipping their brushes in ink or paint and then skillfully wielding them, painters produce on the paper pictures with lines and dots - some heavy, and some light; and some deep, and some pale. In the hands of a good painter brushes and ink can be highly expressive. Because of this, they are seen not only as tools for drawing pictures, but also as a collective symbol of artistic pursuit.

Of the numerous outstanding ancient Chinese painters, many were literati - scholars, officials, etc. - who did not depend on drawing for a living. These people were invariably well versed in the traditional culture - "good at music, chess, calligraphy and painting" as the old saying goes. In fact they developed a unique school of painting, the "school of the literati". The school began rising in the Song Dynasty and became fully developed in the Yuan and, for a time, constituted the mainstream of traditional Chinese painting. Painters of the school drew for self-enjoyment or as a way of self-cultivation, and therefore were not particular about precision or the details of the subjects they were drawing. Instead, the artistic charm of their paintings was what they concerned most. That explains why natural landscapes, birds and flowers were the major themes of those "literati paintings" and why such paintings were often done with simple inking and washing to impress the viewer with a scholarly elegance and taste instead of rich coloring. This artistic style has been influencing painters of all times. The influence has been so strong that at the mere mention of traditional Chinese paintings, people without a full knowledge of this art form would call to mind those ink and wash paintings that feature freehand brushwork.

In comparison to ink and wash paintings, fine brushwork, minute attention to details and rich, elaborate coloring characterize traditional Chinese paintings of a style known as *gong bi zhong cai* that originate from palace paintings. Palace paintings thrived in the Song Dynasty. The country's best painters were grouped in the imperial academy of paintings, where they were ranked the same way as officials according

Part of a Qing Dynasty (1644-1911) painting that visualizes the Grand View Garden in the classical novel *A Dream of Red Mansions*.

The painting brings to life the *Ode to the Goddess of River Luo* by the third century poet Cao Zhi (192-232). Done by Gu Kaizhi (1470-1523), it is recognized as a masterpiece of traditional Chinese painting of the *zhong cai* (heavy coloring) style.

to their artistic accomplishments. For a time in the dynasty, there were schools of calligraphy and paintings to bring up painters and calligraphers qualified for work in service of the imperial family and ranking officials.

Human figures, landscapes, and birds and flowers are the most important themes of traditional Chinese painting. For a long time before the 13th century, priority was given to paintings meant to enlighten the population - those based on religious stories or stories about historic figures, as well as aristocrats and officials in real life. Figures in such paintings, be they may gods, goddesses, deities or people in real life, were invariably urbane and elegant - in fact human figures portrayed in such a way as to conform to ideals of Confucianism. In the 11th century, Chinese painters broke away from this stereotype and began portraying common people in real life in cities or the countryside.

In the late 13th century, figure paintings began declining and giving way to landscape paintings and paintings of birds and flowers. The latter eventually developed into an independent school of fine art, the "flower-bird school". It was named as such because painters of the school liked to do birds and flowers together even though they also did animals, fish and insects. There have always been two dominant styles of bird-flower paintings - those that look magnificent and full of splendor done through rich coloring and with attention to minute details, and those of natural simplicity to impress the viewer with a rustic charm. Palace painters liked to do the former and the so-called "literati painters", the latter.

Landscape paintings constitute the most important - certainly the best known — branch of traditional Chinese painting. The principle of "painting in poetry and poetry in painting" advanced in the 11th century has been guiding landscape painters of all times in their creative work. Landscape painters spare no effort to create a poetic mood in their pictures. A good landscape painting has the magic power to draw the viewer's attention to mountains in the distance and then divert it to those valleys below and, in the end, let the viewer concentrate on trees and streams in the immediate vicinity. Human figures - fishermen, recluses, etc. - are often seen in woods, on mountain trails or sitting beside a lake or a stream. These figures are an indispensable part of the landscape like the rocks, trees, clouds and water bodies, serving to suggest a complete harmony or unity of Nature and man. What is in the background and what is in the foreground are clearly visible in a traditional Chinese landscape painting, and so are what is under the sun and what is in the shade. But the light contrast and the three-dimensional effect are not as explicit as in a Western-style landscape painting. In fact the painter does everything to invoke the viewer's imagination, unlike Western painters whose main task is to present the physical beauty of the scene by using perspective and other techniques.

Traditional Chinese painters portray an object mainly by using lines, especially when drawing human figures. Lines done by competent painters give the viewer a sense of motion, producing an artistic effect somewhat like dancing. Faithfulness "in spirit" is stressed in doing traditional Chinese paintings. In comparison, Western painters do their best to make what they draw look like the real thing. In other words, priority is given to the artistic mood or the "spirit" when a traditional Chinese painting is done, while Western-style paintings look more real. In drawing a human figure, for example, a traditional Chinese painter will not try to make the painted figure look real by following modern

Lone Scholar and Evening Glow done by Tang Yin (1470-1523). Pay attention to words and seal stamps on the upper left part of the painting, which suggest that the painting belongs to the "literati school" of ancient Chinese painting.

anatomical principles. Instead, they will concentrate on details such as the expression in the eyes of the figure and the figure's shape in an attempt to bring out the figure's spirit, temperament and individuality. Painters often project their feelings and thoughts into their paintings of flowers and birds by imbuing them with a spirit of humanity. That's why flower-bird paintings invariably carry a message. Plums, orchids, bamboo and chrysanthemums, which have always been among the most popular themes of the flower-bird school, are seen as embodiments of moral integrity — the "four gentlemen of the virtue" as they are traditionally called. Paintings of these plants, as a matter of fact, imply the pursuit by the painter of moral perfection.

In most cases, traditional Chinese paintings are done with the technique of defocused perspective. The Western technique of focused perspective was introduced to China in the Ming Dynasty, but traditional painters seem to have paid little attention to it. Nevertheless, that does not suggest that traditional Chinese paintings are less charming. As a Western painter once put it, a painting in Western style presents what one sees within the frame of a window, while a painting in traditional Chinese style allows the viewer to see what is beyond the frame. Comments like this certainly do not suggest that the Western technique of focused perspective is inferior — in fact the technique of focused perspective and the technique of defocused perspective each have a merit that the other does not have. But it has to be recognized that the technique of defocused perspective allows traditional Chinese painters the freedom to interpret space and use it in their own way.

Traditional Chinese painters, as a matter of fact, always make sure that enough blank space is left on the paper. A typical example was Ma Yuan of the South Song Dynasty who, in doing a painting, went so far as to just draw on one corner of the paper, hence his nickname, "Ma, the corner". *Angling in the Snowy River*, one of his best-known works, would have been completely blank but for a lone man angling on a small boat. Chinese art critics agree that the blank space is an indispensable part of the painting — in fact the "invisible part of the picture" that inspires the viewer with a desire to "look beyond the

A painting of birds by Huang Quan, known to be active during the Five Dynasties period (907-960). It is recognized as a masterpiece of traditional Chinese painting of the flower-bird school.

visible part". If the blank space on a painting is not large enough to produce such an atheistic effect, the painter would be criticized for having done too much — even for being "unruly" in doing the painting.

Painters often write poems and inscriptions on their paintings and affix their seals to them, and so do collectors of the paintings. The poems and inscriptions are not mere notes on how the paintings were done. Written in different calligraphic styles, these add beauty to the paintings, and so do those seals that are in fact also art pieces. Before doing a painting, a painter will painstakingly plan what to do on this or that part of the paper to make sure that right places are reserved for poems, inscriptions and seals. So traditional Chinese paintings are not "purely" paintings. They are, in fact, art pieces in which fine art, poetry, calligraphy and seal engraving melt into one another for an artistic unison.

Traditional Operas

Traditional Chinese operas, or *xi qu* as known to the Chinese, are recognized as constituting one of the three greatest theatrical schools in the world, along with the Greek and Sanskrit schools. Nevertheless, it is relatively late for the Chinese theatrical school to have become a fully developed, independent art form.

In the course of their development, traditional Chinese operas took their source first of all from what is known as *yue wu* — dancing accompanied by music that dated to remote antiquity. Cross talks and other performances given by palace comedians in the Spring and Autumn period were the second source. Story telling and ballad singing, which are known to the Chinese as *shuo chang,* also inspired the Chinese theatrical school in its development. *Shuo chang* originated from *su jiang*- Buddhist monks preaching teachings of Buddhism by telling stories based on real life - which was popular in the Song Dynasty. Along with the development of handicrafts industry and commerce, by the Song Dynasty there had emerged theaters in their embryo form - the so-called *wa si* — recreational centers in cities. *Wa si* were open all the year round, where people paid for enjoyment over performances of music, singing and dancing, acrobatics, ballad singing, story telling, conjuring, comic talks, etc. As time went by, *xi qu,* a new form of performing art that combines singing, dancing, narration and acrobatic combating to tell a complete story, came into being in the early 12th century.

Classical Chinese operas had its heyday in the Yuan and Ming dynasties. There were countless *xi qu* companies in the country. There were also *xi qu* artists who made a living by organizing themselves into mobile troupes for performance in cities and countryside. Meanwhile, not a few high-ranking officials and noble lords had private troupes performing for their own entertainment. The two dynasties produced a host of playwrights, including many whose plays are still popular today. To cite just a few: Guan Hanqing[5] and his *Injustice Done to Dou Er*, Wang Shifu to whom the *West Chamber*[6] is attributed, and Tang Xianzu (1550-1616) and his *Peony Pavilion*[7].

Beginning as of the late Ming period, however, the focus of the theatrical movement gradually shifted from playwriting to theatrical performances. In the second half of the 17th century, local operas of traditional style began rising - *bang zi* popular in Hebei Province, north China; *huang mei* in Anhui and parts of Hubei, east and central China; *qin qiang* opera in Shaanxi, northwest China; *yue ju* in Zhejiang, east

Hua dan, vivacious young female character in traditional opera.

Lao sheng, aged male character in traditional opera.

China, etc. Today, local operas of more than 300 genres are being performed across the country. These differ from one another in music while featuring words spoken in different local dialects. In 1790, pieces of *hui ju* opera popular in Anhui Province were performed for the first time in Beijing, the national capital. In later years, Peking Opera - often dubbed the "national opera" for its nationwide popularity - came into being as a development of *hui ju* opera and by drawing on the music and techniques of other local operas.

For a long time in the past, traditional operas were performed on stages without curtains, so the audience could watch a performance from three sides. Moreover, there was hardly any stage setting in traditional opera performances. This state of affairs has changed a great deal since the early 20th century when performing artists of Peking Opera in Beijing and Shanghai began performing in modern theaters. Despite change in the venue of performance, the basic techniques — summarized as singing (*chang*), narration (*nian*), acting (*zuo*) and acrobatic combating (*da*) — are still there. Traditional opera performing

artists are so skillful in using body language and dancing movements that even with neither setting nor props, they can make audience "see" that they are opening a door, climbing a mountain, or wading across a stream. Small pieces of stage property are used to enhance the artistic effects generated by largely symbolic movements. By wielding the whip, for example, an actor or actress makes the audience feel that he or she is driving a horse or trying to harness it. Dancing with an oar, he or she shows the audience that a boat is swaying in turbulent waters. The traditional performing art allows the artists maximum freedom to arrange the time and space related to a story. A few warriors on the stage symbolize a huge army. A warrior dancing on the stage in a circle suggests that he is making a journey thousands of miles long.

Stylized movements constitute another salient feature of China's traditional opera art. In fact all movements — opening a window, mounting a horse, stepping onto a boat, etc. — follow fixed patterns, and so do music, plot development, costumes, facial make-ups, etc. Take the colors of facial make-ups, for example. Red is the color for loyal and gallant characters; black, for those who are upright; and white, for those who are vicious and crafty. On seeing the color and the pattern painted on the face of a character, the audience will automatically know what kind of a person he or she is.

Singing, Dancing and Acrobatics

Thousands of years ago, ancestors of the Chinese nation created a unique art form in which performers sang poems set to music while dancing. As time went by, poetry broke away and became an independent literary form. But singing and dancing have always come together as one traditional art form.

During the early period of China's recorded history, sacrificial and court ceremonies always proceeded amid performances of *ya yue* — a combination of instrumental and vocal music with dancing arranged in such a way as to fit in with the solemn and majestic atmosphere characteristic of such occasions. *Ya yue* was meant to eulogize the virtue of the sovereign. Meanwhile, it played a role of "education" or "enlightenment" by impressing the people with the might of the sovereign. As a matter of fact, it was an indispensable part of the social hierarchy. In the Zhou period, for example, the number of performers in *ya yue* ensembles was stringently fixed for the "son of the Heaven" and the dukes and princes under him, and so were the contents of the songs, the tones of the music, and the musical instruments used in ceremonies. As the power of the "son of the Heaven" kept declining, the hierarchical rites came to be ignored in the Spring and Autumn

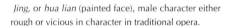

Jing, or *hua lian* (painted face), male character either rough or vicious in character in traditional opera.

period. This made it possible for court artists to adapt folk music and dancing for performance at court ceremonies.

In all dynasties of ancient China, palace music and dancing were the mainstream of singing and dancing. In the Han and Tang dynasties, China enjoyed an unprecedented economic prosperity and its economic and cultural exchanges with foreign countries boomed as a result. This ushered in the heyday of China's traditional singing and dancing. The governments of both dynasties had offices in charge of collecting folk songs and music and training singers and dancers while responsible for formulating rules and regulations concerning performances. Emperor Xuan Zong of the Tang, who reigned from 712 to 756, was himself a composer while good at playing a variety of musical instruments. He set up an imperial theater called *"li yuan"* — in fact China's first school of music, dancing and performing art — where he personally took up teaching to several hundred trainees. Music of the dynasty exerted a profound influence on the development of Chinese music and literature. The most striking example was *qu zi ci* — "poems set to music" — developed in the dynasty, which by the Song Dynasty had developed into *ci*, a major form of classical Chinese poetry.

In the 13th century, *xi qu* — story telling through singing and dancing that was to develop into traditional operas — became popular as the major form of public entertainment. Singing and dancing as an independent art form became less important as a result. But, they have continued to exist as an indispensable part of traditional opera and, as such, have followed rules left over from the past in arrangement and

A set of 65 bronze musical bells excavated from a tomb of the Chu Kingdom more than 2,000 years ago. The set is still good enough to play music with.

performance.

China's traditional musical instruments date to ancient antiquity. In the West Zhou period, for example, musical instruments in more than 70 varieties were already in use. Experts tend to classify these into eight types according to the materials they were made of — instruments of metal, stone, wood, bamboo, silk strings, etc. which, in terminology of Chinese musicology, is referred to as *ba yin* or the "eight types of musical sound". The West Zhou period produced China's earliest musical bells of bronze. From a 2,300-

Enjoying the Music of Qin (qin is a traditional plucked instrument). Zhao Ji, one of the Song Dynasty (960-1279) emperors, did the painting. The musician is the emperor and the men listening are his ministers.

year-old tomb in Suixian County, Hubei Province, archeologists found a set of 65 musical bells. These bells are divided into eight groups according to their sizes and the pitches of the sound they are able to produce. Hung from a three-layer frame three meters high, the bells, when struck, produce a range consisting of five octaves along with all the 12 semitones for each — good enough to play any music like piano. The tomb is indeed an underground music hall, from which 27 other instruments were also excavated, including drums, *se*[8], *qin*[9], *sheng*[10] and pai *xiao*[11].

Traditional Chinese instrument music falls into two major types, *si zhu yue* (ensemble of stringed and woodwind instruments) and *chui da yue* (ensemble of wind and percussion instruments). The word *si zhu* can refer to any traditional Chinese music, but a typical *si zhu* ensemble consists mainly of *zheng*[12], *sheng*, *pipa*[13] and flute. The kind of *si zhu* orchestras consisting of *qin*, se and wind instruments had served mainly to accompany dancing and singing before it became able to give concerts. Music by this kind of *si zhu* orchestras is popular mainly in south China. It is exquisite and elegant in style and often features a mood of ease and liveliness. Such orchestras are usually small, sometimes consisting just of a few *er hu*[14] and flutes. In comparison, *chui da* orchestras are large and usually perform in the open. *Chui da* music is unrestrained in style, depicting scenes or feelings of jubilation. Generally speaking, wind instruments play the leading role in *chui da* music popular in the north, in comparison to *chui da* music popular in the south that stresses the role of percussion instruments. In the past, traditional orchestras performed at weddings and funerals and in the course of idolatrous processions while indispensable at court ceremonies, and musicians gave relatively few solos. Things have changed a great deal over the recent decades, and the country has produced numerous soloists of traditional music instruments who are popular in China and have won a fame in the world.

Lively and unrestrained, Chinese folk dancing has always been popular. That may explain why many ancient folk dances have been preserved to this day while court dancing has largely been reduced to oblivion. Folk dancing seems more popular in the countryside than in cities, but on festival occasions, cities are also a scene of jubilation when people dance out in public places. Classical Chinese dancing features a combination of skills and artistic grace. A good example is

"Musicians".

West Han Dynasty (206BC-24AD) "acrobats" who are performing to the accompaniment of an "orchestra".

the Lion Dance left over from ancient times, which is in fact a performance of dancing, acrobatics and martial art. As special skills are required in performance, folk dancing like the Lion Dance has to be done by people trained for that. People of China's ethnic minority groups seem to be better in dancing than people of the Han majority. All Tibetans are dancers, their dancing reputed for a beauty of primitive simplicity with upward swaying of the arms and forcible stamping of the feet. Mongolian dancing clearly mirrors the group's nomadic life on the grassland - horse racing, cow milking, etc. In comparison, slow, graceful movements characterize dancing of the Zhuang and Li groups who inhabit farming areas in south and southwest China, which is in fact based on activities in real life such as picking tea leaves and husking rice.

From Han Dynasty tombs dating to the period from the second century BC to the first century AD, archeologists have found numerous brick relieves depicting performers and performances of conjuring and acrobatics as well as of music, singing and dancing. Unlike their Western counterparts who play with the aid of acoustic and optical props, Chinese magicians can produce things out of the blue just by wearing a traditional long robe or shaking a piece of cloth. Brick relieves

Tang Dynasty music and dancing depicted on a mural on one of the Mogao grottoes. Note the dancer holding the plucked instrument *pipa* behind her head.

of the Han suggest that more than 2,000 years ago, China already had a rich repertoire of acrobatics requiring highly difficult skills to perform, including balancing a long pole on the head, climbing a long pole, dancing on a tight rope and throwing summersault through a circle. Chinese acrobats have always attached great importance to training in basic skills of using muscles of the legs and waist and of balancing loads of incredibly heavy or easy-to-break things on the head.

During the Three Kingdoms period, a mechanical toy of cams, connecting rods and gears was invented. Driven by a fall of water, the wooden prime mover gear would drive various figurines to "perform" - "actresses" dancing, beating a drum or playing flute, and "male acrobats" throwing knifes, standing on their heads on a tight rope, etc. The toy testified not only to how popular acrobatics had become in China, but also the level of mechanical engineering the country had attained.

Some props used in performance of Chinese acrobatics are also worth mentioning. According to Professor Joseph Needham (1900-1995) of Britain, a top authority in ancient Chinese science and technology, it is the umbrella used by Chinese tightrope dancers for balancing that inspired the invention of parachutes.

1. A poem of four lines, each containing five or seven characters, with a strict tonal pattern and rhyme scheme.

2. A form of classical Chinese poetry written to certain tunes with strict tonal patterns and rhyme schemes, in fixed numbers of lines and words, which originated in the Tang Dynasty and became fully developed in the Song.

3. A type of verse for singing, which emerged in the South Song and Jin dynasties and became popular in the Yuan.

4. Some of China's ethnic groups do have epics rated as literary and historic treasures. The Tibetans, for example, are always proud of King Gessar, an epic that has been passed on orally to this day.

5. Guan Hanqing was born in the late Jin period and died in the early Yuan period. The *Injustice Done to Dou Er*, also known as *Snow in Midsummer*, tells the story of how an innocent woman is wronged and executed. It has been acclaimed as a vehement protest against the feudal society and its officialdom.

6. Wang Shifu lived in the Yuan Dynasty, but the exact years of his birth and death are not known. In the *West Chamber*, the hero, a young scholar, and the heroine, a high class girl fall in love with each in defiance of the feudal ethical code under which marriages were always arbitrarily arranged for young people by the family elders.

7. The *Peony Pavilion* is a story of love between a young scholar and a high-class girl. The girl meets her lover in dream. She dies of frustration but returns to life later and gets married with her lover she once met in dream.

8. A 25- or 16-stringed plucked instrument, somewhat similar to the zither.

9. A seven-stringed plucked instrument, also similar to the zither.

10. A reed pipe instrument.

11. Panpipes.

12. A 21- or 25-stringed plucked instrument.

13. A plucked string instrument with a fretted fingerboard.

14. A two-string instrumrnt.

Diverse Beliefs in Harmony

Diverse Beliefs

An established religion is invariably unique in itself, claiming to be the ultimate representative of truth. It may be interesting, however, to note that in China, different religious beliefs have always co-existed in harmony. Side by side with Taoism, the indigenous national religion, are Buddhism, Islam and Christianity that originated from foreign lands. Confucianism, which exerted a dominating ideological influence in ancient times, is often referred to as *ru jiao* - literally meaning the "religion of Confucianism" - though in a strict sense it is not a religion.

Ancient China was tolerant to all religious beliefs, irrespective of

Mural in one of the Mogao grottoes in Dunhuang, Gansu Province. Most Dunhuang grottoes tell Buddhist stories.

Part of the Qing Dynasty (1644-1911) folk painting *Deities of the Three Realms,* in which the Supreme Master of Taoism, Sakyamuni of Buddhism and Confucius are treated as equals.

their origins, indigenous or alien. Buddhism was born in what is now India but has been unable to take a firm root there. In the West, religions are invariably exclusive, each following a set of commandments and doctrines that demand total allegiance on the part of believers. A European, for example, cannot believe in two religions at the same time, and neither can the person be a member of two different sects of the same religion. In ancient China, however, people seemed quite indifferent toward the differences in commandments and doctrines of different religions. Because of this, Taoism, Buddhism and *ru jiao*, which were dubbed as the "three greatest beliefs", were all able to constantly grow in strength and influence while melting into one another. Beginning as of the Tang Dynasty, something that combined the "three greatest beliefs" was to develop and eventually come to represent a historic trend in ancient China. Under such circumstances, a person could be a believer of both Taoism and Buddhism while a faithful follower of Confucian teachings. Ancient Chinese showed the same amount of respect for the Supreme Master[1] of Taoism, the founder of Buddhism, Sakyamuni, and the Chinese sage Confucius. The *Deities of the Three Realms,* a folk picture that can still be seen in remote, outlying rural areas, is a convincing proof to religious equality and harmony characteristic of China's religious culture. In the picture, the Supreme Master of Taoism, Sakyamuni of Buddhism and Confucius each have a place in the highest of all heavens, suggesting that the three beliefs are equal and that their followers live side by side in peace.

Other cultures are rarely as tolerant as the Chinese culture to alien beliefs. This tolerance is, of course, conditional, in that all religions, indigenous or alien, must show due respect for China's traditional social ethics and must in no way do harm to the secular power. Provided this condition is strictly followed, rulers of all ancient Chinese dynasties would willingly allow different religious belief to spread. Generally speaking, the rulers of a dynasty would allow a religion to exist and recognize its legitimacy even though they themselves did not believe in it. It is therefore safe to say that religious freedom or tolerance has been a part of China's cultural tradition since ancient times.

In ancient times, religions existed side by side with worshipping of Nature, awe in ancestors and superstitious reverence for the supernatural. Official sacrificial ceremonies were held regularly under the personal auspices of the emperor to beg the heaven, earth, sun, moon and proceeding emperors of the dynasty for blessings so that the dynasty would continue to exist, forever in peace, order and prosperity. Confucius was honored at government-sponsored sacrificial ceremonies held in all cities and towns. The Spring Festival, the most important Chinese festival that falls on the first day of the lunar year, was the occasion for families to offer sacrifices to their ancestors at private memorial services. This was also the occasion for sacrificial offerings in honor of the various deities supposedly to protect families from disasters or misfortune - the Door God, the Kitchen God, the Water Well God, the God of the Earth, to name just a few. Ancient Chinese believed that gods and deities each had the "duty" to protect a specific place or industry. A city, for example, was under the protection of *cheng huang,* the "Town God". Carpenters believed that Lu Ban, the most prestigious carpenter in the Warring States period, became their divine protector after he died.

Song Dynasty (960-1279) statue of the Buddhist Goddess of Mercy in a grotto in Dazu County, Sichuan Province.

Buddhist statue in one of the Tang Dynasty (618-907) grottoes in Mt. Maiji, Gansu Province.

Buddhism

Buddhism found its way from India into China in the first century AD by taking the Silk Road. At first, it was taken simply as a sort of witchcraft. Despite that, the religion was able to steadily build up its influence in the country. It boomed in a historic period spanning from the third century to the sixth, a period when the country was torn apart by incessant wars and social upheavals. Unable or unwilling to face the harsh reality squarely and for mental relief, the literati and officialdom turned to *xuan xue* - a philosophical sect of metaphysics that had something in common with the philosophical approach of Buddhism. The spread of Buddhism gathered momentum as a result and the number of Buddhist believers in all social strata snowballed. The period of the North and South Dynasties from the early fifth century to the late sixth, in particular, saw Buddhist temples spring up everywhere with support from some of the top rulers.[2] While growing in numbers, Buddhist temples became economically powerful by owning large areas of farmland given them by governments or rich people. And along with the spread of Buddhism, there emerged numerous schools of Buddhist theology, each taking a specific classic of Buddhism as its central philosophical text.

Buddhism had its heyday in the Sui Dynasty that succeeded the Northern and Southern Dynasties and the Tang Dynasty that succeeded the Sui. In both Sui and Tang dynasties full religious freedom was guaranteed. Defying untold hardships, Monk Xuan Zhuang (602-664) of the Tang Dynasty left Chang'an (what is now Xi'an), the Chinese capital, in the year 629[3] and went all the way to India to study Buddhist classics. He came back 19 years afterwards, bringing with him 650 volumes of Buddhist sutras in Sanskrit. On imperial orders he settled in Chang'an, and devoted the rest of his life to translating these sutras into Chinese. While promoting Buddhism, he founded the *Fa Xiang* or the *Dharmalaksana* sect that advocates the supremacy of consciousness with a view to promoting Buddhist idealism. As time went by, Monk Xuan Zhuang became a legendary figure. Based on legends about him, the 16th century writer Wu Cheng'en wrote the *Pilgrimage to the West*, one of the four greatest classical Chinese novels.

To secure a foothold for their religion in China, Buddhists spared no effort to compromise Buddhist doctrines and commandments with secular laws, disciplines and moral standards and, in the process, the religion became an important part of the Chinese culture. A range of

Tripitaka (Buddhist texts) Pavilion at Guiyuan Monastery of Wuhan, Hubei Province.

Portrait of Tsong-kha-pa (1357-1419), founder of the Yellow Sect of the Tibetan school of Buddhism.

Pilgrims in front of the Jokhang Monastery in Lhasa, Tibet.

schools of Chinese Buddhism came into being. Of these, the *Chan* or *Mahayana* sect - known as Zen Buddhism in Japan — founded in the early Tang Dynasty was to develop into the mainstream of Chinese Buddhism. Followers of the sect believe that *Buddhata*, or the virtuous nature of the Buddha, is present in everybody heart, and that everybody can be a Buddha provided he or she becomes imbued with *Buddhata* through self-cultivation. On the basis of that understanding, the sect stands for enlightenment by direct intuition through meditation. In other words, one can attain utter perfection without having to learn Buddhist sutras by heart or perform those elaborate religious rituals.

Buddhism found its way into Tibet in the seventh century, and was eventually to develop into Lamaism - the Tibetan school of Buddhism - through centuries of struggle against Ben, Tibet's primitive religion while compromising with its merits. Kublai (1215-1294), or Emperor Shi Zu of the Yuan Dynasty, conferred on Phatspa (1235-1280), a most revered Tibetan lama, the honorific title "National Teacher" and designated him to administer religious and secular affairs in Tibet. This suggested establishment of a government combining political and religious powers that was to rule the region until the democratic reform in the 1950s, after the founding of the People's Republic of China.

Then came Tsong-Kha-Pa (1357-1419), founder of the Yellow Sect that was to develop into the mainstream of Tibetan Buddhism. Over the centuries, Lamaism has been the most important religion in regions inhabited by ethnic Tibetans including the entire Tibet Autonomous Region and parts of Sichuan and Qinghai provinces, and it is also the religion of ethnic Mongolians who inhabit what is now Inner Mongolia Autonomous Region.

Taoism

Taoism, as a religious belief, began rising in about the second century. As a religion, it had its heyday in the seventh century when China was under the Tang Dynasty. Taoists attributed the founding of their religion to Lao Zi, whose real name, however, was Li Er. As luck would have it, the imperial family of the Tang Dynasty was named Li. In a bid to show that the imperial power was divine-given, Emperor Xuan Zong claimed that Lao Zi or Li Er was his family's ancestor and, because of this, he spared no effort to promote Taoism.

The truth, however, is that as an independent religion, Taoism came into being on the basis of several religious groups which, though organizationally independent of one another, all drew on Lao Zi's Taoist philosophy for spiritual inspiration. While striving for development of their religion, Taoists enriched it also by borrowing from craft of ancient necromancers to ward off disasters and keep health, as well as witchcraft and other superstitious practices. As time went by, Taoists melted other ingredients into their religion, most prominently the Confucian ethic standards of loyalty to the sovereign and filial piety for the elder and the Buddhist belief in *samsara* or transmigration. The highest pursuit of Taoists is to attain the Tao[4] and become immortals. Their immediate concern, however, is to keep fit and live a long, healthy life.

In the initial stage of development, Taoism had a popular base, so popular that it was connected with some of the peasant uprisings. Beginning as of the Wei-Jin period in the third century, however, the religion drew increasingly close to the ruling class and came to serve the feudal court, as some Taoists tried to curry favor with the monarchical regimes in a bid to promote the religion. These Taoists took the task of begging heavenly blessings for the monarchical regimes and seeking ways to make members of the rulings class immortal. Meanwhile, a popular form of the religion came into being and became increasingly popular among ordinary people seeking to protect themselves from diseases, disasters and misfortune. Taoism is polytheist, and it worships countless gods, goddesses and deities, each supposedly performing a specific function or duty. The Dragon King, for example, can be counted on for rain. One may go to Lord Guan for protection from disasters and misfortunes. The God of Medicine is supposedly to have magic power to make patients recover. If you want to get rich, well, beg the God of Wealth for blessing. Ma Zu Goddess, the protector of sailors and travelers sailing the turbulent seas, has been worshipped not only in China's coastal regions but also by overseas Chinese in practically all parts of the world. In ancient times,

Taoist immortals as depicted in a mural at the Yong Le Temple in Ruicheng County, Shanxi Province.

numerous Taoist temples were built on imperial or government orders, mainly in cities and other population centers. Temples dedicated to different gods, goddesses or deities built by people themselves can be found even in the most remote areas of the country. As time went by, religious practices melted into folkways and local customs, many of which are still followed.

In the past, Buddhist and Taoist temples were invariably land and property owners, and their incomes consisted mainly of rent payments and donations from believers. From time to time emperors granted them land and other rewards as a token of official recognition of the religions.

Islam

Islam was brought into China in the mid-7th century. Arab and Persian merchants who came for business played a big role in promoting the spreading of the religion in the country. This was true especially in the Song Dynasty when trade between China and Arab countries flourished. Quanzhou of Fujian and Guangzhou of Guangdong had the largest Muslim communities in China who, comprising merchants and imams from the Arab world, took advantage of the government policy of religious freedom to build mosques and spread Islamic teachings. Muslim communities there were able to expand fast along with a steady increase in the number of inter-marriages between Arab immigrants and local Chinese. Still larger numbers of Muslims — mostly soldiers and handicraftsmen — came to China from Central Asia, Persia and Arab countries after Mongol armies under Genghis Khan started a westward expedition in the 13th century. These immigrants, who were referred to as "Hui Hui" in the Yuan Dynasty, were found everywhere in China. By the time the Ming Dynasty replaced the Mongol regime, the "Hui Hui", through cultural intercourse and marriages with people of the Hans, the Mongols and people of other ethnic groups, had developed into an independent ethnic group called "Hui". As a social group, the Huis took the spread of Islam as a holy duty. When China was under the reign of the Tang and Song emperors,

A mosque in Xinjiang.

Muslim communities in China were, in general, social groups of autonomy that paid relatively limited attention to spreading Islam among outsiders. In the Yuan Dynasty, however, spreading of Islam became an organized social activity and, as a result, the religion was able to exert a growing influence on the development of Chinese society.

Ten ethnic minority groups in China now take Islam as their religious belief, including the ethnic Huis who live in almost all parts of the country, and Uyghurs and Khazaks who are found mainly in Xinjiang. China's ethnic groups believing in Islam have a combined population of 17 million.

Christianity

Relative to Buddhism and Islam, Christianity followed a somewhat tortuous course as it spread in China. In the early 7th century, the Christian sect of Nestorianism found its way into China. The Nestorian Tablet, the oldest relic of Christianity in China, is now displayed in the Forest of Tablets — a museum of ancient stone carvings in Xi'an of Shaanxi Province. It was set up in Chang'an -- what is now Xi'an

A Western missionary working with a group of Chinese women. The photo was taken in the late Qing period.

— in 781 as a token of thanks to emperors of the Tang Dynasty for the courtesy they afforded to Nestorian priests and believers. Emperor Wu Zong of the Tang Dynasty of the mid-9th century, however, changed the policy of religious freedom and closed down or demolished large numbers of Buddhist, Taoist and Nestorian temples. Nestorianism began to decline and eventually came to extinct in most parts of China after the 10th century.

In the late 13th century, Christianity was introduced to China for a second time, and was able to recruit believers — mostly from among members of upper class Mongols. But before long, it came to extinct with the collapse of the Yuan Dynasty. Christianity made a comeback again in the 16th century — pioneered by missionaries of the Roman Catholic Church of whom Jesuit missionaries were to become most influential. Matteo Ricci (1552-1610), an Italian Jesuit missionary, was a most outstanding representative of the missionaries from the West. He arrived in China in 1582 and, before long, became a friend of the imperial family and many aristocrats of the Ming Dynasty. To facilitate their missionary work, Matteo Ricci and other missionaries from the West helped the imperial observatory revise the traditional calendar, build firearms and spread scientific knowledge. According to historic records, the number of Chinese Christians had grown to 300,000 by 1701. Nevertheless, Christian concepts and doctrines were in direct conflict with the values and practices of Confucianism — the most essential part of China' traditional culture — and the country's folkways. Western missionaries, with Matteo Ricci as representative, stood for tolerance towards practices like worshipping of the Heaven and the ancestor and, in fact, tried their best to reconcile Christian commandments with Confucian teachings. This touched off a heated debate between the Jesuits and other sects of Roman Catholic Church. In 1704, the Holy See issued an order prohibiting Chinese Christians to worship the Heaven and their ancestors. In response, the Ming government banned missionary work in China.

Christianity once again found its way into China by taking advantage of the colonialist expansion by Western powers. The gunboat policy pursued by Western powers forced China to sign a series of unequal treaties beginning as of the mid-1880s. Missionary work became legal under protection of these treaties. Consequently, conflicts between Christianity and China's traditional values sharpened, and so did contradictions between Western missionaries and the Chinese people, culminating in the Boxer's rebellion towards the end of the 19th century. Beginning as of the early 20th century, Western missionaries changed their ways of promoting the religion in China by means of charity work such as starting schools, hospitals, etc.

Ru Jiao as the Core of China's Traditional Values

Ru jiao, the so-called "religion of Confucianism", comprises a complete set of Confucian philosophical approaches and ethical standards. It is the core of their traditional values. For this reason, the Chinese are not as addicted to religious beliefs as some other peoples and, consequently, never has a religion been able to become the national religion. In contrast, Confucianism was the dominant ideology for well over 2,000 years. During this period, no other political and social philosophy was able to challenge its supremacy and no religion was influential or powerful enough to replace it.

The Confucian culture calls for a rational approach towards society and life, and that explains why relative apathy towards religious belief constitutes a salient feature of the Chinese culture. Religions took a dominant position in Europe over a prolonged period from the fourth to the 14th century. More often than not, there were sharp differences between the church and secular regimes and between different sects of the same religion. Theologies rode high above secular politics, laws, philosophies and ethics, and countries even fought bloody wars for the sake of religious beliefs. In China, however, it would be beyond even the wildest imagination that a religion could someday become powerful enough to ride above the imperial power and the state. Never has China had a religious leader in a position as high as Pope. Neither has the country had the kind of social mechanisms that made it possible for state policies to be based on God's will or commandments. In the period of the North and South Dynasties and later centuries, every dynasty had a central government organ that took charge of religious affairs. The supreme rulers of all dynasties were invariably tolerant towards religions

Sculptures of Sakyamuni, founder of Buddhism, and his disciples at the Zhengguo Temple, Pingyao County, Shanxi Province.

while trying to make use of them. In most cases, they were impartial in handling differences and disputes between religions and, from time to time, acted as "judges" trying to mediate a settlement. When Buddhism had its heyday, virtually all Buddhist temples were wealthy owners of land and other property. This made it possible for monks and nuns to lead a parasitic life on incomes of their temples even though they accounted for a significant part of the population. In view of what they saw as an economic threat plus misgivings about the religion, on three occasions emperors of the Tang and some of the preceding dynasties ordered suppression of Buddhism by closing down Buddhist temples, confiscating their property and forcing monks and nuns to resume secular life. Nevertheless, none of the crackdowns was long or severe enough to drain the religion of its strength. Besides, not a single religious conflict of a massive scale occurred in ancient China.

The Buddhist Baby-Giving Goddess: The statue exemplifies the old belief that more children mean more happiness.

Unlike religions, Confucianism calls for attention to worldly life - politics, ethics, etc. and in no way does it stand for pursuit of happiness in the other world or of things that are preeminent above real life. It is true that Buddhism flourished in the Tang and Sui dynasties. Nevertheless, it was able to play a role in society just by providing people in distress with kind of mental relief, and it was Confucianism that people continued to count on for principles guiding all aspects of social life. When Neo-Confucianism was established in the Song and

Ming dynasties, Confucianism restored its position as China's predominant ideology.

The secular nature of Confucianism influenced Buddhism and Taoism in their development. Buddhist commandments and doctrines, which stress salvation of one's soul rather than the duties one should perform in society and one's responsibilities for the family, collided head-on with the traditional Chinese values that are essentially family-oriented. Moreover, disobedience to the sovereign and reluctance to perform one's filial duties were cardinal crimes under China's feudal, monarchical system of government. So Buddhism was forced to compromise itself with Confucianism by declaring allegiance to the monarchy and obliging its followers to perform their filial duties. Meanwhile, Buddhists spared no effort to make far-fetched comparisons between Buddhist and Confucian values — between Buddhist commandments and ethical standards of Confucianism, to be more precise. Without much trouble, Buddhism melted into China's dominating belief in both theory and practice.

Debates broke out intermittently between the three beliefs — Confucianism, Buddhism and Taoism. Buddhists were always clear about the supremacy of Confucianism. Their debates with exponents of Confucianism were not meant to challenge the supremacy of Confucianism, but to affirm the legitimacy of the religion. By engaging in debates with Taoists, Buddhists were trying to win a higher social position for their religion by attaching it to Confucianism and by proving that its doctrines and commandments were more rational. In other words, such debates were meant to win over the public. Through debates with Buddhists, Taoists reaffirmed their allegiance to the monarchy by attaching Taoism to Confucianism — the same way as Buddhists did — while drawing on some of the Buddhist doctrines, rites and practices.

Religious Buildings

In ancient India, grottoes were in fact Buddhist temples comprising clusters of caves. Often there were small chambers built by digging

Azure Cloud Temple, a Taoist shrine, atop
Mt. Taishan in Shandong Province.

into the walls of a grotto, in which monks stayed for meditation. In
some grottoes there were pagodas for worshipping by Buddhist
believers, and in front of them there were squares where believers
gathered for religious ceremonies.

Though originating from India, Chinese grottoes, many of which
have been preserved to this day, are different in design and structure.
Buddhist statues were placed in shrines built by digging into the walls
of a grotto and murals on Buddhist themes were painted on the walls.
In front or at the side of a cluster of grottoes a temple would be built.
The Mogao Grottoes of Dunhuang in Gansu Province, the Yungang
Grottoes of Datong in Shanxi and the Longmen Grottoes of Luoyang
in Henan are reputed across the world as treasure houses of Buddhist
art. Buddhist statues and murals in those grottoes are visual
documentation of immeasurable importance to studies of ancient
China's economy, religion and architecture as well.

The earliest Buddhist temples in China invariably had a pagoda in
its center. Changes in temple design took place under the influence of

the indigenous architectural art and, by the Sui-Tang period, halls had replaced the pagodas as the main structures in a temple. And since then, halls have been where Buddhist statues are displayed for worshipping and monks gather for sutra chanting. Many temples have a courtyard special for pagodas, which is either behind the main courtyard of the temple or at the side of it. A keen observer can easily find that a Buddhist temple resembles the palace complex or a typical government office in ground plan. The gate, the main halls for display of Buddhist statues and the sutra-chanting hall sit astride the axis of the temple, which are flanked by less important buildings — the drum and bell towers, monks' dormitories, etc. All buildings in a temple are in neat rows, which are linked by long corridors. In areas inhabited by people of minority ethnic groups like Tibet and Yunnan, Buddhist temples are built in styles quite different from those built by the Han majority. This is because Tibetans and the Dais in Yunnan, as ethnic minority groups, follow different sects of Buddhism and their architectural art is also different.

Images of Buddhist gods and goddesses have, over the centuries, also undergone changes to become a part of the Chinese art. The earliest Buddhist figures as statues and portrayed in paintings were Indian, pure and simple. But before long, facial expressions and bearings characteristic of ancient Chinese were becoming increasingly explicit in Buddhist statues and paintings done by Chinese artists. Indian gods and goddesses now came to be "clothed" in Chinese daily wear, with the lines done in such a way as to resemble those characteristic of traditional Chinese figure paintings. In fact the closer the areas where these alien images were done are to China's heartland, the more will the images look like Chinese. In classical scriptures of Buddhism, *Avalokitesava* is a lieutenant or disciple of the Buddhist patriarch in the Land of Ultimate Bliss. In China, *Avalokitesava,* who is described as gender-less in Buddhist classics, was "transformed", roughly in the 6th century, into Guan Shi Yin — the Goddess of Mercy who will instantly rush to the rescue of any person in distress on hearing the person's cry for help. Guan Shi Yin or the Goddess of Mercy seems to

A Protestant Church in Qingdao City,
Shandong Province.

have since then enjoyed a higher regard than Sakyamuni, the Buddha patriarch. Over the centuries, statues and portraits of Guan Yin — invariably beautiful while holy with a bearing of benevolence — have been displayed for worshipping in practically all temples and countless homes. What happened to *Avalokitesava* in China proves that though an alien religion, Buddhism became assimilated with the secular life as it spread in the country.

Taoist temples have the same architectural style as the traditional palace complexes or government offices. These are mostly found in mountains and other sites that are secluded but reputed for scenic beauty — in places that Taoists believe can help them avoid the worldly and hold themselves above the vulgar so that someday, they will, by practicing asceticism, become immortals.

Mosques and other Islamic monuments built in China before the Ming Dynasty are predominantly Arab structures. Along with the spreading of Islam since the Ming and Qing dynasties, mosques that look like structures in traditional architectural styles have sprung up in many places. Mosques in Xinjiang Uyghur Autonomous Region,

A mosque in Tongxin County, Ningxia Hui Autonomous Region. Note the traditional Chinese architectural style of the structure.

however, still retain their Arab originality.

Christianity is the last of the alien religions to have settled in China, and churches in China are largely of the same architectural style as those in the West.

1. This is the honorific title for Lao Zi, to whom the *Scripture of Ethics* (*Dao De Jing*), the central text of Taoist doctrines, is attributed.

2. A typical or extreme example was Emperor Wu Di (464-549) of the Liang, one of the Southern Dynasties. A fanatic believer of Buddhism, he stayed in Buddhist temples as a monk for three separate periods to promote the religion.

3. Some historians hold that the monk left Chang'an one year earlier.

4. In the Taoist philosophy, the formation Tao means the Way of Nature that cannot be given a name.

Traditional Chinese Medicine and Pharmacology

Yin-Yang and the "Five Elements"

Achievements made by Ancient Chinese in natural sciences are, by and large, no longer in practical use, having been replaced by the modern scientific system developed in the West. The only exceptions are perhaps traditional Chinese medicine and pharmacology that form a unique scientific system. In ancient times, traditional medicine and drugs were the only means to treat diseases and protect people's health. Today, the Chinese still have faith in them even though Western medicine is practiced everywhere.

Traditional Chinese medicine and pharmacology take the ancient ideas of *yin-yang* and *wu xing* (the "five vital elements") as the theoretical basis in striving to explain the various physiological and pathological

A doctor of traditional Chinese medicine and his patient as depicted in a Qing Dynasty painting. Pulse feeling is a basic diagnostic technique in traditional Chinese medicine.

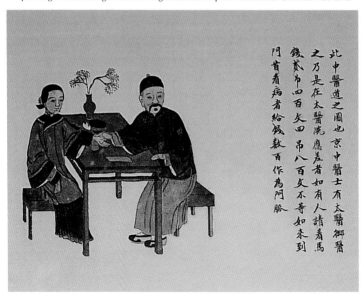

The Chart of the Heaven, Earth and Nature. The blank part of the circle symbolizes *yang*, and darkened part, *yin*. The words round the circle denote different periods of the evolution of Nature.

phenomena and their interactions. These form a complete scientific system unique in both theory and practice, consisting of interconnected elements in physiology, pathology, pharmacology and in prevention, diagnosis and treatment of diseases.

Ancient Chinese held that the universe is formed with two kinds of *qi*[1] called *yin* and *yang*, and that it is the interplay of these two opposing principles of nature that spark all changes and movements in the universe. The concept of *yin-yang* was originally used to refer to the direction of the two sides of the same subject in relation to the sun – the side facing the sun is *yang* and the opposite side, *yin*. As time went by, the *yin-yang* concept became increasingly broad in meaning – *yin* referring to things static, cold, dark, descending or inward while *yang*, to things dynamic, warm, bright, ascending or outward. Classification of things that way just represents the philosophical approach of unity of the opposites, and in no way is it meant to differentiate what is good from what is bad. People also made farfetched comparisons between *yin-yang* and the various social and natural phenomena – *yang* being whatever is masculine and *yin*, whatever is feminine, for example. Ancient Chinese held that the interplay of *yin* and *yang* is the fundamental law governing all changes and movements in the universe — spring replacing winter, boon in bane and bane in boon, etc. Harmony was seen as the most ideal state for the universe and society. Only when the *yin* and *yang* – the various forces in the universe or society — are in perfect equilibrium or unity can the universe and society maintain a proper order.

The *yin-yang* concept has also become the theoretical premise of traditional Chinese medicine. Take, for example, some of the physiological functions of the human body. According to the *yin-yang* concept, excitation suggests that the human body is in the state of *yang* and, when the human body is in the state of *yin*, depression will be the inevitable result. *Yang* predominates during daytime, which is also the time when the human body is mainly in the state of excitation. *Yang* turns into *yin* after dark and that's why people retire to bed at night. The human body, in fact, is seen as the universe in miniature. When the *yin* and *yang* elements in the body of a person are well balanced, the person is in good health, and the person falls ill when this balance is disrupted.

The concept of *yin-yang* is closely associated with the concept of *wu xing* – the "five elements" (metal, wood, water, fire and earth). Ancient Chinese believed that the physical universe comprised these five elements. The five elements are interlocked in set patterns according to their natural relationships, exerting a generative and, at the same time, a subjugative influence on one another. That is to say that each is generated while subjugated by a different one. Wood generates fire, fire generates earth, earth generates metal, metal generates water, and water generates wood. Meanwhile, wood subjugates earth, earth subjugates water, water subjugates fire, fire subjugates metal, and metal subjugates wood. It is through this generative-subjugative cycle of the five elements that the physical universe or nature maintains a dynamic balance, a balance that manifests itself, for example, in the change of the four seasons every year.

Like the *yin-yang* concept, the concept of *wu xing* also constitutes a fundamental theoretical premise of traditional Chinese medicine. Each vital organ is seen as belonging, by nature, to one of the five elements – the heart belongs to fire; the liver, to wood, the spleen, to earth; the lungs, to metal; and the kidneys, to water. The five vital organs are interlocked in the same kind of generative-subjugative relationships, and it is believed that a pathological change in any of the vital organs inevitably results in abnormal function of other vital organs.

The five vital organs in traditional Chinese medical theory do not

Medicinal materials being processed – paintings left over from Ming Dynasty (1368-1644).

conform exactly to Western anatomical science. They are taken as the five vital systems of the human body, and these systems are connected with other organs of the body by *jing luo* – a network of main and collateral channels through which *qi* or the vital energy circulates. For example, the ears are connected with the kidneys through *jing luo* and the eyes, with the liver. *Jing luo* is neither the system of blood circulation nor the system of nerves. Modern anatomical science has failed to physically identify this web of collateral channels supposedly branching out to all parts of the human body. But its existence can be verified through laboratory tests.

Human diseases are diverse, and pathological changes are found not only in the five vital organs. According to theories of traditional Chinese medicine, the heart is the "chief of the vital organs" that regulates the other organs through blood circulation, and pathological changes, no matter where, invariably have something to do with this or that vital organ. The human body is a unitary whole and, when the functions of an internal organ are disrupted, the symptoms can be discerned in the complexion, eyes, color, voice and texture of the tongue fur, etc. By analyzing these indicators, the doctor will know what is wrong with the patient.

Over the past 2,000 years and more, physicians of traditional Chinese medicine have always used four basic methods of diagnosis: *wang* (observing), *wen* (listening to the patient's voice and smelling the patient's odor), *wen* (interviewing) and *qie* (feeling the pulse of the patient). The order of business in such diagnostic process is first for the patient to describe the chief complaints and more obvious symptoms of his or her ailment. The physician will then ask the patient to open his or her mouth wide to examine the texture of the tongue fur. Meanwhile, the physician will carefully observe the patient's complexion, skin color, etc. and ask the patient to explain when, where and how he or she first fell ill, what symptomatic changes have taken place from the onset right up to the day he or she visits the physician. Then pulse diagnosis will follow. The physician places his or her first three figures along the radial artery of the patient's wrist, feeling for three specific points. Light pressure on these points reveals three separate pulses, while heavy pressure reveals yet three different ones, a total of six pulses on each wrist. Each of the 12 pulses reveals the conditions of an organ. The pulse qualities – "floating", "sunken", "weak", "bounding", etc. – indicate conditions of the related organ. With skilled, sensitive figures, the Chinese doctor can detect more than 30 different kinds of pulse quality on each of the 12 pulses.

Traditional Chinese medicine has a long history, being the accumulated experiences of the Chinese people in their millennia-long struggle against diseases. *Huang Di Nei Jing* (the *Yellow Emperor's Canon of Medicine*), also known simply as *Nei Jing* (the *Canon of Medicine*), is the earliest and most comprehensive medical classic from both the theoretical and clinical points of view. Compiled in the third

Illustrations of some medicinal herbs in *Ben Cao Gang Mu* (*Compendium of Materia Medica*) by Li Shizhen (1518-1593) of the Ming Dynasty.

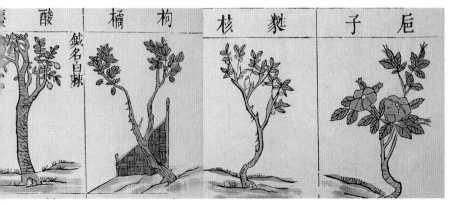

century BC, it has been recognized, in particular, as the central theoretical text of traditional Chinese medicine. The fundamental theories and clinical experiences of traditional Chinese medicine are so closely related to each other that one could never be a competent physician without a full understanding of the *yin-yang* and *wu xing* theories, which, as we have mentioned, are philosophical approaches as well.

Traditional Chinese pharmacology and acupuncture and moxibustion

Traditional Chinese pharmacy consists mainly of natural medicinal materials – plants, animal parts and minerals of medicinal value as well as some chemical compounds and biological drugs. Chinese historians attributed the discovery of herbal medicine to the legendary Emperor Shen Nong who is believed to have lived in the New Stone Age. So wrote Sima Qian, a Han Dynasty historian: "Shen Nong tasted the myriad herbs, and so the art of medicine was born". In trying those herbs on himself, he is said to have got poisoned 70 times in just a single day, but each time he found the right kind of detoxifying herbs to save his own life. What is said of Shen Nong is, after all, just legendary, but it can easily be imagined that pioneers of traditional Chinese medicine must have risked their lives in finding out what herb was good for what illness.

A qualified Chinese physician must know the medicinal and therapeutic value of each and every medicinal material from among hundreds and even thousands used to treat diseases. Around the second century BC, *Shen Nong Ben Cao Jing (Shen Nong's Materia Medica)* appeared as China's earliest pharmacological work. It dealt with 365 medicinal herbs divided into three categories. Hundreds of pharmacological works were compiled in the later centuries, either by private researchers or under government auspices. The most important, however, is *Ben Cao Gang Mu (Compendium of Materia Medica)* by Li Shizhen (1518-1593) of the Ming Dynasty. Completed in 1852, the encyclopedia contains not only descriptions of 1,892 medicinal materials with illustrations but also 11,000 prescriptions in 16 parts. It has been republished again and again and translated into numerous languages.

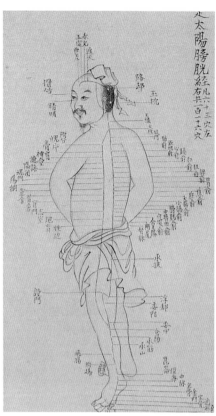

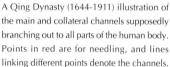

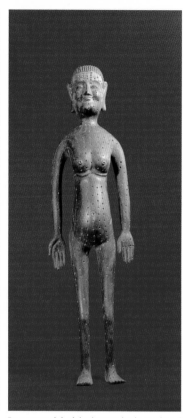

A Qing Dynasty (1644-1911) illustration of the main and collateral channels supposedly branching out to all parts of the human body. Points in red are for needling, and lines linking different points denote the channels.

Bronze model of the human body produced in the Qing Dynasty (1644-1911) for medical training. Note the *xue wei* or acupuncture points inscribed all over the model.

Until now, Chinese experts have identified the therapeutic value of more than 8,000 medicinal materials. Of these, there are more than 6,000 species of medicinal plants.

Medicinal herbs must be collected in the right time of the year, when they have the best therapeutic and medicinal value. In most cases, herbs and other medicinal materials are processed before they are used as ingredients of decoctions. Pots of the right kind – usually pottery – are used to prepare decoctions with, and the different ingredients are put into the pot for boiling in following the order prescribed by the doctor.

Moreover, attention must be paid to ensuring the right duration and degree of heating as ordered by the doctor. The most important thing, of course, is the prescription. There are different prescriptions for different diseases and even for the same disease prescriptions may vary from patient to patent according to the specific conditions of each. The country has produced numerous doctors known in and outside the country for their skills. For proven effectiveness, many ancient prescriptions are still in clinical use. Prescriptions by famous doctors of all ages are invariably compiled into books to be passed on from generation to generation as textbooks for students of traditional Chinese medicine.

As we have already mentioned, modern anatomical science has failed to physically identify the web of main and collateral channels supposedly branching out to cover the entire body, but its existence can be verified by using scientific instruments. In fact practitioners of traditional Chinese medicine have never questioned the existence of the *jing luo* system, convinced by the effectiveness of acupuncture, as well as by *qi gong* (a system of breathing exercises) and other traditional ways of keeping health.

Many millennia ago, the Chinese already knew that pains could be relieved and some diseases could be cured by stimulating certain points on the body. These points were to be called *xue wei* – points for acupuncture and moxibustion – which are believed to exist on or beyond the main and collateral channels called *jing luo*. So in addition to medication, doctors of traditional Chinese medicine treat diseases by needling *xue wei* or heating them usually with fire of mugwort leaves. Acupuncture needles are specially made for treatment of diseases. As the human body is a unitary whole with different parts connected by a web of *jing luo* channels and collaterals, pains in a certain part of the body can be relieved or cured by needling or heating a point far away from it. Clinical experiences have proved that the treatment is effective for numerous illnesses, especially for various kinds of pains, sensory disturbances and dyskinesia. Along with the development of modern sciences, electric, magnetic, laser, infrared-ray and microwave devices have been developed to stimulate the *xue wei* or acupuncture points for

Chinese shadow boxing.

treatment of diseases.

Ancient practitioners of traditional Chinese medicine produced myriad works, including monographs, on *jing luo,* acupuncture points, acupuncture needles and their clinical use, diseases that can be treated by acupuncture and moxibustion and what the patient should abstain from in receiving acupuncture treatment. There were also many charts illustrating the distribution of *jing luo* channels and collaterals and acupuncture points. What merit special mention are two bronze models produced under the supervision of imperial doctor Wang Weiyi of the 11th century. The models were inscribed with a web of *jing luo* channels and more than 300 acupuncture points. They were used for training and examination of acupuncturists. The examinee was asked to puncture the figure that was filled with mercury, and the acupuncture points were coated over with wax. Whether or not the mercury leaked would determine the accuracy and precision of the examinee's puncturing.

In addition to treating diseases, acupuncture can be used in local and

Illustrations of *wu qin xi* – or the "five mimic-animal boxing" conducted by imitating the motions of the tiger, deer, bear, monkey and bird.

even general anesthesia. Acupuncture anesthesia makes it possible for patients to be operated on with little pain while perfectly sane, and it is good especially for patients on whom anesthetics cannot be used. Acupuncture anesthesia comes as a latest development of the acupuncture art of treatment, as an achievement practitioners of traditional Chinese medicine have made by combining the traditional Chinese and Western medicines. The birth and development of acupuncture anesthesia has contributed to studies of *jing luo* and other theories of traditional Chinese medicine and, at the same time, inspired modern physiology, biochemistry and anatomy with questions worth of painstaking research.

Like acupuncture and moxibustion, massage is popular in China as a method of treatment without use of drugs. It is highly effective in treating sprains, contusions, pains in the legs and waist and numbness.

Traditional ways of keeping fit

Traditional ways of keeping fit have always been popular among the Chinese, who believe that prevention of diseases is more important than treatment.

Like the traditional Chinese medicine and pharmacology, traditional ways of keeping fit date to remote antiquity. One hard proof is *dao yin tu* – a chart on a piece of silk cloth excavated from a Han Dynasty tomb 2,000 years ago that depicts a complete set of more than 40 gymnastics to promote health and cure diseases by combining physical exercises with self-massaging and regulated, controlled breathing. Hua Tuo (145-208), the renowned late Han Dynasty physician, developed a set of exercises called *wu qin xi* – or the "five mimic-animal boxing" conducted by imitating the motions of the tiger, deer, bear, monkey and bird.

To live a long, healthy life, the Chinese have been keen to traditional ways of maintaining physical and metal soundness by leading a regular life, taking the kind of diet that best fits their conditions, and doing *wu shu* and *qi gong* exercising.

Qi gong, a general term referring to different sets of regulated, controlled breathing exercises, originates from *dao yin.* Sets of *qi gong* exercises can be divided into two types, the dynamic and static types, according to the strength used to conduct the movements; or into the kind of exercises just for keeping fit and the kind of exercises for curing diseases. There are different schools of *qi gong* exercises – medical *qi gong*, religious *qi gong*, martial art *qi gong*, etc. if classified by taking into account the different cultural forms they assume. *Qi gong* is subject to diverse interpretations, but it is generally believed that it lets the body and mind to regulate their functions in a completely natural state of relaxation and ease. On the basis of Chinese *qi gong* that found its way into the West in the 20th century, European and American doctors have developed a variety of new therapies – the auto-breathing therapy of Germany, the relaxation and meditation therapies of the United States, etc.

Wu shu, or *kong fu* as better known in the West, was in fact a kind of martial art for hand-to-hand combats in ancient times. In modern times, however, people do *wu shu* just for exercise. There are two types of *wu shu* — free-handing *wu shu* and *wu shu* done with weapons. Boxing is the core of free-handing *wu shu,* and is also the basic skill of *wu shu* done with weapons, hence the saying "training of a *wu shu* master begins with boxing". There are different schools of Chinese boxing. Some feature imitation of animals' motions – the monkey boxing, snake boxing, eagle's claw boxing, etc. *Mian quan* or the school of "soft boxing" features slow, stretching movements to limber up one's muscles and joints. *Zui quan,* the "drunkard's boxing" – is a set of exercises imitating a person's reeling under the influence of alcohol. When speaking of a versatile person, the Chinese like to say he or she is "skilled in using each and every of the 18 weapons". The proverb derives from *wu shu* done with weapons, the figure, 18, suggesting that many kinds of weapons are used in martial art – broad swords, swords, spears, cudgels, etc.

Wu shu and *qi gong* are closely linked to each other, hence the saying "without a proper training in *qi gong* one will never master the art of *wu shu*". A typical example of this combination is the Chinese shadow boxing known as *tai ji quan,* which features high concentration of the mind and slow, regulated breathing that accompanies the rhythmical motions of the arms, legs and body. As a kind of exercise, it is good especially for the aged and those who are physically weak.

Let nature take its course – that is the principle that has been guiding the Chinese in doing different kinds of exercises to keep fit. That means doing everything within the limit of one's physical strength. Besides, it is believed, one must never indulge in sensual pleasure. Not a few Chinese emperors died of poisoning after taking drugs prepared with certain minerals – mercury, for example, which they had believed would make them immortal. This made people believe that to keep fit either through medication or exercising, one must never do anything without proper guidance.

Bequeathing of traditional Chinese medicine.

Traditional Chinese medicine is unique, in that even today, it still exists side by side with Western medicine while most other nations have lost their medical traditions. This can be attributed to a variety of factors, most prominently the continuation of the Chinese culture since ancient times. Largely empirical, traditional Chinese medicine has survived the test of times thanks to practice of physicians of one generation after another, and to those ancient medical works that record their theories, skills and practical experiences.

As a unique system of concepts, theories and methods, traditional Chinese medicine is entirely different from Western medicine in premises and principles. It treats the human body's physiological functions as an integral whole, as an inseparable part of the universe of Nature and society, and sees the different organs as inherently bound by an inter-relationship. It is from this understanding that stems the theory of pathology that attaches a great importance to relationships of the disease a patient suffers with his or her physical and mental conditions, the various natural and social conditions in which the patient lives in, the climate in particular. Unlike Western medicine that prefers to deal with structural concepts, fixed quantities and rigid laws, traditional Chinese medicine, in clinical practice, attempts to cure diseases by helping the patient restore the balance of *qi* in different vital organs. In other words, it aims at treating the principal and secondary aspects simultaneously, instead of taking only palliative measures for an illness. Besides, drugs and decoctions of traditional Chinese medicine are made up of natural materials, and stringent procedures are followed in their preparation.

sword dancing.

Chinese boxing.

Because of this, extremely limited toxic and other side effects are observed in their clinical applications.

A least a thousand years ago, traditional Chinese medicine and pharmacology were introduced to Vietnam, Korea and Japan. Western medicine came to China in the Ming Dynasty. Since the 19th century, attempts have been made to integrate the merits of traditional Chinese and Western medicine. In modern China, there are hospitals using methods of both to diagnose and treat diseases, in addition to hospitals "purely" Western or Chinese.

1. The major premise of Chinese medical theory is that all the forms of life are animated by an essentially life-force vital energy called *qi*. *Qi* also means "breath" and "air", similar to the Hindu concept of *prana*. Invisible, tasteless and odorless, *qi* nonetheless permeates the entire cosmos.

Chinese Calendars and Festivals

Traditional Calendars

Ancient Chinese astronomy dealt mainly with calendrical science, unlike astronomy of Europe that has always concentrated on study of celestial bodies. The history of Chinese calendrical science is a long one. The earliest calendars, only fragmentary evidences of which are extant, are believed to date to the Xia period more than 4,000 years ago, and that is how the traditional lunar calendar came to be known also as the "Xia Calendar". In the Shang period, there was already a complete calendrical system. It divided the year into 12 months, consisting of longer months of 30 days and shorter months of 29 days that kept occurring alternately. While dealing with the arrangement of the years, months and days, the calendar told people of the changes in farming seasons — when to sow the seeds and when to harvest the crops.

The traditional Chinese calendar is lunar-solar in nature. The solar calendrical science is based on solar movements, in which the duration of time for the sun to move from one Spring Vernal equinox to the next is counted as one tropical year. The lunar calendar, however, is based on the law governing the waxing and waning of the moon. Ancient Chinese took the day the moon disappeared from view as the first day of the lunar month. They called the day *shuo,* and the day the moon becomes full was referred to as *wang.* The time from one day of *shuo* to the next day of *shuo,* or from one day of *wang* to the next day of *wang,* was counted as one synodical month. The tropical year and the synodical month are the basic constants. By the Spring-Autumn and Warring States periods, the Chinese calendar had already been brought to a very high degree of perfection. In the quarter-remainder calendar used then, a tropical year consisted of 365.25 days and a synodical month, of 29.53025 days. But the 12 synodical months had a total of 354 days, roughly 11 days short of the tropical year' actual duration. To resolve that problem, ancient Chinese calendar makers of the sixth century began applying the principle of seven intercalations in every 19 tropical years, a system that came to be known to the Western world only 200 years later.

It is on the basis of the quarter-remainder calendar that the traditional Chinese lunar calendar was to become fully developed through repeated reforms. Guo Shoujing (1231-1316), the renowned scientist of Yuan Dynasty, set the tropical year at 365.2425 days in his *Shou Shi Li* (*the Official Calendar*), with an error of only 26 seconds from the actual time with which the earth makes one revolution round the sun. *Shou Shi Li* matches the Gregorian Calendar in accuracy. People of today are using the Gregorian Calendar, but few know that 300 years before the Gregorian Calendar came into being, the Chinese had already done something as perfect.

All ancient Chinese calendars are closely associated with agricultural production. Ever since the third century BC, the traditional Chinese calendar has divided the year into 24 *jie qi* or solar terms. These terms, which directly refer to the ecliptic positions of the sun, are good indicators of the season. As the terms are based on the ecliptic positions of the sun, the day each *jie qi* begins is relatively fixed in the Gregorian Calendar. The term *gu yu* (grain rain), for example, begins roughly on April 20 by the Gregorian Calendar, when weather turns warm and rainfall becomes increasingly frequent – time for Spring sowing and growth of over-wintering crops. *Xia zhi,* the summer solstice, falls on June 22, the day summer begins in the north hemisphere. This is the season when all plants – crops and weeds alike – grow fast, hence the farmers' saying, "weeds of *xia zhi* in cotton fields, as vicious as venomous snakes", which is in fact a timely call for weeding and pest control. The system of the 24 *jie qi* or solar terms serves as a practical guidance for farm work, and that's why the traditional Chinese calendar is also called *nong li* or "agricultural calendar".

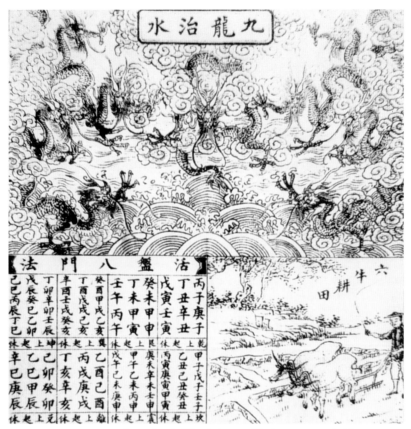

A page in a traditional almanac. Words on upper part of the page read "we have nine dragons to control flooding" and words on the lower part, "we have six oxen to plough the fields".

Astronomical Observations

Today, everybody knows that changes in ecliptic positions of the sun and the moon, the twinkling of the stars and appearances and disappearances of comets are nothing but natural phenomena. In ancient China, however, people always linked these natural phenomena to political changes and outbreak of social chaos or epidemics, regarding them as God-given omens or warnings. Because of this, almost every Chinese dynasty had an imperial observatory with a full-time staff

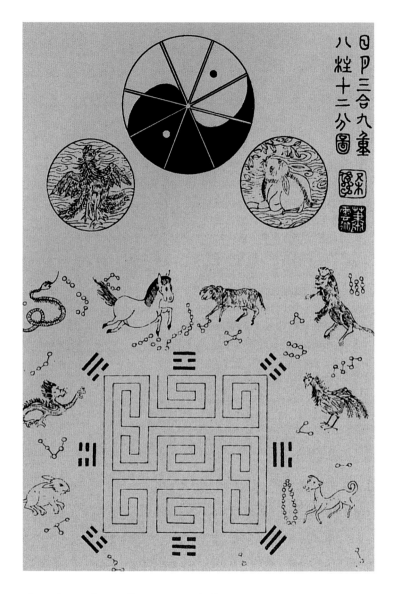

observing and recording astronomical events.

    Ancient Chinese astronomers produced a complete documentation of solar eclipses. Far back in the Yin-Shang period, descriptions of solar eclipses were already cut on oracle bones and tortoise shells. From the year 720 BC to the year 1872 AD, a total of 985 solar eclipses

◀ Produced in the Qing Dynasty (1644-1911), the Chart of Heavenly Riddles may well be seen as a concentrated expression of how ancient Chinese saw the universe. On the top of the chart there is the Diagram of the Heaven, Earth and Nature, with the blank part of the circle symbolizing *yang* and darkened part, *yin*. At either side below the chart there is the sun (left) and the moon (right). According to legend, the sun is an immensely huge crow that is always burning but never dies, and the moon is the habitat of an immortal rabbit. The labyrinth suggests how, as ancient Chinese saw it, the different types of terrain is distributed on earth and in what directions. Round the labyrinth are eight *ba gua* combinations of three whole or broken lines with which ancient Chinese tried to explain changes in the universe and human society. And round the combinations are 12 animals symbolizing the 12 periods into which the day is divided.

were recorded in history books of different periods. Of these, only eight had wrong dates or were impossible to verify by using modern scientific knowledge. In Chinese classics there is also a wealth of descriptions of sunspots, comets, meteors, meteorite showers, novae and supernovae. French philosopher Voltaire spoke highly of ancient China's astronomical achievements, noting that among people of all nations, only the Chinese had a compete documentation of solar and lunar eclipses, documentation verified by European astronomers as almost perfectly authentic.

In fact forecast of solar and lunar eclipses was an important part of ancient Chinese astronomy. Even in remote antiquity Chinese astronomers already viewed solar and lunar eclipses as something occurring alternately and according to a fixed pattern. Basing themselves on this understanding, they were able to calculate, by using a calendar, when a solar or lunar eclipse would occur, and then they would verify the accuracy of their forecast through observation. If the calculation proved to be incorrect, they would set about revising the calendar. Calendrical revisions not only promoted the development of astronomy, but also opened a new horizon for development of mathematics. Ancient Chinese were good at different branches of mathematics, algebra in particular. Moreover, they had to their credit the invention of abacus using the decimal counting process. Extremely complicated calculations can be done with an abacus, and the speed can be faster than with a modern calculator when simple calculations like additions and reductions are done. That's why abacus was able to find its way into Japan, Southeast Asia, Central Asia and West Europe, and has been used since ancient times, even in the current computer era.

The Heavenly Stems and Earthly Branches

It is less than 100 years since China came to adopt the Christian system to number the years. Before that, how did the Chinese do that?

Before the Han Dynasty, there were different ways of designating the years. During the Warring States period, for example, ways of designating the years differed from state to state. The system of *gan zhi* — heavenly stems and earthly branches – was adopted in the Han Dynasty some 2,000 years ago, and has been used ever since. *Gan* refers to *tian gan* – the ten heavenly stems named separately as *jia, yi, bing, ding, wu, ji, geng, xin, ren* and *gui*. These are actually signs of a serial order. *Zhi*, the abbreviation of *di zhi*, refers to the 12 earthly branches, namely, *zi, chou, yin, mao, chen, si, wu, wei, shen, you, xu* and *ha*i. The earthly branches indicate the 12 two-hour periods into

Abridged armillary sphere developed by Guo Shoujing (1231-1316), a renowned scientist and astronomer of the Yuan Dynasty.

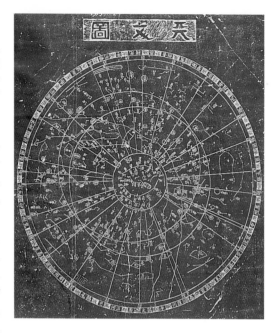

Star map engraved on an ancient stone tablet. Some 1,434 fixed stars, along with the Galactic System, was marked on the map produced 1247.

which the day was traditionally divided. For example, *zi* refers to the period from 23:00 hours to 1:00; *chou*, to 1:00 to 3:00; and so on and so forth. The 10 heavenly stems and 12 earthly branches form a system of designating the year. The first heavenly stem and the first earthly branch, when put together, indicate the first year, which is referred to as the year of *jia zi*. Then there are the year of *yi chou*, the year of *bing yin*, and so on and so forth until the 11th earthly branch comes to pair with the first heavenly stem, forming a 60-year cycle that goes round and begins again

This way of designating the years is certainly not good enough for practical use. Suppose something happened in a year of *jia zi*. As the 60-year cycle goes round and begins again infinitely, people decades or centuries later would find it difficult to figure out to which cycle that particular *jia zi* year belonged. The problem was resolved in 140 AD, when people began using both the *gan zhi* system and imperial reign titles to designate the years.[1]

Since ancient times, the Chinese have used 12 animals to symbolize the 12 earthly branches – the rat, cow, tiger, rabbit, dragon, snake, horse, sheep, monkey, cock, dog and pig. These animals also sympoblize the year in which a person is born – Mr. Wang was born in a year of the tiger, and Miss Li was born in a year of the rabbit, etc. It may be interesting to note that in old times, from these symbolic animals superstitious and fatalist practices stemmed. Even if Mr. Wang and Miss Li truly loved each other, their families wouldn't let them marry, insisting that there would be no peace when a "tiger" lived with a "rabbit".

Traditional Festivals

There are hundreds of traditional festivals in China. No wonder so many – the country is so large, its history so long and its population so diverse in ethnicity and culture. Festivals of the various ethnic groups often enliven the folkways of their ancestors. Meanwhile, festivals of ethnic groups invariably have something in common as they are all rooted in the traditional Chinese culture.

In Europe and West Asia, most festivals are religious or inspired by religious beliefs, and religious ceremonies are therefore an important part of festival celebrations. In China, however, most festivals, festivals of the Han majority in particular, have little or nothing to do with religions. Their birth and development have been closely related to agricultural production, worshipping of ancestors and, in some cases, to primitive taboos. Many festivals reflect the way of life in an agricultural society. The most important festivals always feature reunion of families and elaborate rituals in honor of ancestors – a concentrated expression of the traditional social ethics characteristic of the Chinese nation. There are also festival activities supposedly to

Comets painted on a piece of silk, produced at about 350 BC.

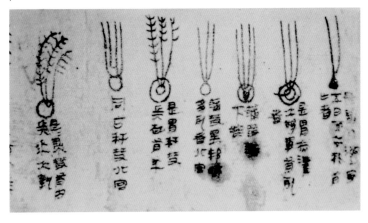

A Qing Dynasty (1644-1911) folk painting, depicting a family receiving friends and relatives during the Spring Festival.

ward off evil spirits and misfortune and usher in happiness and good luck for families and individuals.

Traditional Chinese festivals are designated according to the traditonal lunar calendar. The Spring Festival is the most important of all festivals, the festival for the vast majority of the Chinese, for Chinese living anywhere in the world, in or outside the country. It falls on the first day of the lunar new year, a kind of thanksgiving for the good harvest in the past year and for happiness and peace in the new year. Days before the festival, families will clean their houses, in hope to see off the old and welcome in the new. Then antithetical couplets written on bright red paper are put up on doors. These "spring festival couplets" invariably are composed of auspicious words — "all crops are good", "the livestock thrive", etc. For merchants, the most favorite couplet reads "the four seas thrive with business, and the three rivers overflowing with wealth." Portraits of the so-called "Door God" will be put up on gates and doors to ward off any evil spirit. Also popular are those "new year paintings" done by folk artists, which depict scenes and images with auspicious themes such as good harvest, long lives and peace.

Famliy reunions feature the eve of the Spring Festival. When midnight arrives, people of all generations in a family will have the festival feast together. Before gunpowder was invented, people would burn fresh bamboo for the sound of cracking, which they believed would scare evil spirits away. The tradition continued after the invention of gunpowder, the difference being that people set off firecrackers instead of burning fresh bamboo. Modern Chinese set off firecrackers just to increase the festival atmosphere. But in recent years, Beijing and a few other cities have banned setting off of firecrackers in downtown areas for concern of fires and injuries and for control of noise pollution. In old time, families would hold elaborate rituals in honor of their ancestors. This tradition has faded out in modern times but exchanges of visits between friends and relatives have always been an indispensable part of the Spring Festival repertoire, as have been gala parties at which the dragon, lion and *yangko* dancing and walking on stilts are performed amid the sound of beating of drums and gongs.

The comes the *Yuan Xiao* Festival on January 15 on the lunar calendar to celebrate the first full moon in the new year which, as the Chinese see it, symbolizes family reunion. *Yuan xiao* – also known as *tang yuan* — are round sticky rice balls with a sweet filling, which are

Putting up the auspicious character 福 (pronounced as fu, meaning "happiness") written on bright red paper or in paper-cuts is still the way of celebrating festivals and weddings.

Old customs die out slow. Even today, people in the countryside still like to put up couplets and portraits of household guardians on their doors.

sufficiently boiled in water for eating. In addition to eating of *yuan xiao*, the festival features lantern parties in the evening, and that's why the festival is also known as the "lantern festival". Dispay of lanterns dates to Emperor Ming Di of Han Dynasty who ruled China from 56 AD to 75 AD. The emperor, who was a pious follower of Buddhism, ordered lanterns to be lighted in his palace and temples for Buddha worshipping the day the first full moon for the new year appeared. As time went by, display of lanterns that evening became a folk custom and, to enhance the joyous atmosphere, people often wrote riddles on lanterns for guessing by family members or friends.

Qing ming, which arrives two days before or after April 5 by the Gregorian Calendar, is one of the 24 *jie qi* or solar terms, the time for sowing of crop seeds and tree planting. As a festival, however, it is time for people to pay tribute to graves of dead relatives, or go outing to enjoy the sun and greenery of early spring.

The *Duan Wu* Festival falls on May 5 by the lunar calendar. According to textual research by historians, in remote antiquity it was the festival in honor the dragon. The legendary animal was the totem for people inhabiting areas on the lower reaches of the Yangtze River, where people offered sacrifices to it on that festival. But in later centuries the festival became dedicated to Qu Yuan, a great patriot and

Dragon Boat Race, a Qing Dynasty (1644-1911) painting. One of the streamers in the painting bears the characters meaning "a long, long life to his majesty", prompting the assumption that the race is being held to celebrate the emperor's birthday.

poet. Qu Yuan, of the third century BC, was a high minister of the State of Chu. He was devoted to his country and people but the king, fatuous and self-indulgent, disliked him. A staunch advocate for resistance against aggression by the State of Qin in the north, Qu Yuan was deprived of his power and sent into exile. Frustrated for inability to help his country when the Qin armies captured its capital city, Qu Yuan drowned himself in the Miluo River in what is now Hunan Province. On hearing the news, people gathered where he died and threw *zong zi* – pyramid-shaped pies made of glutinous rice wrapped in bamboo or reed leaves – into the river, in hope that dragons in the river would be lured away from his body. As time went by, May 5 by the lunar calendar developed into a national festival for eating of *zong zi* and dragon boat races. In many parts of China, the festival is also the occasion for people to hang stacks of calamus and Chinese mugwort leaves on the lintels of their doors and spray realgar liquor in and outside their houses. This habit stems from the ancient belief that the smell of the plants can expel poisonous insects, and the liquor can keep snakes off from houses. No wonder. At this time of the year, the weather is getting hot and insects and snakes have all fully awakened from their winter sleep.

The Mid-Autumn Festival, also known as the "Moon Festival", falls on August 15 by the lunar calendar, in the wake of the summer harvest. There is the theory attributing the festival to ancient rituals for moon worshipping, but it is also believed that the festival originates from a sort of thanksgiving in honor of the God of the Earth for the harvest people have just got in. No matter how diverse the theories are, whatever people do in celebration of the festival is closely associated with the moon. Families would gather to enjoy the silvery full moon on the festival evening while eating "moon cakes". As the Chinese see it, the full moon – the moon cakes as well — symbolizes "fullness of the family". Ever since ancient times, there have been countless essays and poems describing how the moon inspires longings for home.

The Double Ninth Festival, which falls on September 9 by the lunar calendar, is the traditional occasion for mountain climbing and

Emperor Xian Zong during the Lantern Festival, a Ming Dynasty (1368-1644) painting, depicts celebrations of the Lantern Festival in the Forbidden City.

enjoyment over chrysanthemum flowers. In ancient times, on that day people would drink wine with chrysanthemum flowers soaked in it, believing that one would enjoy a longer, healthier life by drinking the so-called "chrysanthemum wine" or eating raw chrysanthemum flowers. The fruit of medicinal cornel was also indispensable for the festival. It was placed everywhere in and outside houses to expel mosquitoes.

There are numerous other festivals for people of the Han majority. People of ethnic minority groups all have their own traditional festivals, which are as diverse and colorful.

1. The year 1900, for example, was a *geng zi* year. Historians often designate that year as the "26th year of the reign of Emperor Guang Xu of the Qing Dynasty.

In Pursuit of Good Luck and Happiness

Auspicious Animals and Birds

The Chinese have had their own ways to express their longings for good luck and happiness. These longings, strong and ardent, are manifested in every aspect of their life, in those auspicious words, propitious days, lucky numbers, auspicious animals, etc. Even in modern China, pursuit of good luck and happiness, which takes a deep root in the Chinese culture, remains an important part of the Chinese people's inner world.

The Chinese have taken many animals as auspicious, but the legendary dragon has always been the most important and popular. In the West, the dragon has always been pictured as a fire-spitting demon often with more than one head, in fact as the most vicious, most ferocious thing. In China, however, the dragon turns out to be something with the divine power to bestow upon people happiness, something that invokes the greatest awe and highest respect in the minds of the Chinese people.

According to a most popular assumption, the Chinese dragon was born in the course of the evolution of different totems. Indeed, the legendary animal combines the body parts of many real animals which, in remote antiquity, may have been worshipped as totems. It has the antler of the deer, the head of the horse, the eyes of the rabbit, the ears of the rat, the body of the snake, the scales of the fish and the claws of the eagle, while its feet look like those of the tiger. Believing that the dragon can mount the clouds and plunge into the sea to summon wind and rain, ancient Chinese built numerous temples dedicated to it, in hope that the legendary animal would bestow upon the earth timely wind and rain for the crops.

Beginning as of the Han Dynasty, the dragon, the dragon bright yellow in color in particular, became the symbol of the imperial power – nay, the very symbol of the emperor. The supreme rulers of the Han and all the following dynasties claimed that they were the personifications or incarnations of the dragon and that they were under divine protection by the dragon. So the dragon came to be associated with whatever had anything to do with the imperial power or the emperor. The dragon robe, for example, was meant for the emperor only, and so was the "dragon chair" as the one in the Hall of Supreme Harmony in the Forbidden City of Beijing

While special for emperors, the dragon nonetheless had profound folklorist implications and was seen by the people as a most important auspicious animal. Images of the legendary animal can still be seen everywhere in the country. In ancient times, the dragon for the people was different from the dragon for emperors only in color. As has been mentioned, dragon designs bright yellow in color were for the emperor exclusively, while those in artworks or popular activities — such as in dragon dancing and dragon boat races – were mostly red or green. Dragon dancing and dragon boat racing are still popular, and the dragon remains a favorite theme for creative work of modern Chinese artists. But the legendary animal is no longer feared and has long been cut off from politics. The dragon is now taken as the symbol of the Chinese nation, the symbol of the national pride of the Chinese people, who call themselves "the descendants of the dragon".

The legendary bird, phoenix, is often paired with the dragon. The phoenix, so the legend goes, is the "queen of all birds". Like the dragon, it combines the characteristics of many animals and birds. But unlike the dragon, it is the symbol of virtue and beauty. The phoenix roosts only in Chinese parasol trees, drinks only from the Divine Spring, and eats nothing but bamboo — one of the plants taken as symbol of great virtue. It was believed that the country would be in peace and good order under a wise sovereign when the auspicious bird descends from the Heavens. The phoenix used to symbolize the imperial power the same way as the dragon. But as time went by, the dragon and the phoenix came to be assigned gender-based roles. In the Ming and Qing dynasties, phoenix designs and patterns were meant for women. In the Ming Dynasty, the wives of officials at the ninth and higher grades were obliged to wear phoenix coronets when attending important events. Like the dragon, the phoenix has always been a favorite of the common people. In a traditional wedding, the bride invariably wears a bright red silk robe with phoenix designs embroidered on it.

While visiting the Forbidden City in Beijing, a careful observer can't miss those bronze statues of *qi lin* or the Chinese unicorn in front of the most important halls. The animal, with the body of the deer and the tail of the bull, symbolizes benevolence and virtue. According to legends, the strange-looking animal descends from the Heavens only when the country is in perfect peace and when government administration is sound and wise. In old times, both the sovereigns and people liked it, believing that in addition to bestowing peace upon the earth, the legendary animal, when begged, would send babies to couples. Old traditions die out slow, indeed – even today, folk artists are still producing pictures showing chubby, colorfully

Glazed dragon on a wall in an imperial palace garden.

dressed children riding on the back of the animal. In old times, wedding gifts and gifts for births invariable bore its image.

The tortoise is one of the four greatest "divine animals", the other three being the dragon, phoenix and unicorn even though it is real, not legendary. The tortoise has a very long life, prompting the assumption that it must be experienced and knowledgeable. That explains why back in remote antiquity people were using tortoise shell as the tool of divination. So the real animal became somewhat legendary and, because of that, it attained a high "status". In the Han Dynasty, official seals of gold had a buttonhook in the shape of a tortoise. For some years in the Tang Dynasty, tortoise-shaped ornaments of gold, silver or copper were badges denoting different official rankings.

Stone or bronze lions are often seen in front of structures left over from ancient times – palaces, temples, residences, mausoleums, etc. While "guarding" a courtyard or a hall, the fierce-looking animal was meant to symbolize the power of its owner and the inviolability of that power. Despite that, lion dancing has always been popular which, like the dragon dancing, is performed on festival occasions to increase the joyous atmosphere.

The tiger is often referred as the "king of all animals", and seen as the symbol of strength, might and health. People regard the tiger as an auspicious animal that protects them from disasters. In old times, parents or grandparents would let a baby boy wear the "tiger-head cap" and "tiger-head shoes" when his first birthday was celebrated, in hope that the baby would be as strong as the tiger while free from any disaster or physical injury. Then the baby would be dressed this way on his birthday of every year until he grew into a teenager. In shape, the shoes, usually made of yellow cloth, are embroidered with a design of a tiger head on each, the lines on the forehead forming the Chinese character 王, which means "the king". The "tiger-head cap" is made the same way and has the same connotation. In some parts of north and northwest China, a woman often receives a pair of tigers made of flour dough on her wedding – obviously symbol of a hope that she will produce a male baby as strong as a tiger cub.

Copper-plated iron lion in the Forbidden City.

The red-crested crane is known as the "divine crane", which is also a symbol of long life. According to legends, immortals fly by riding on "divine cranes". Cranes are often painted together with pines – one more symbol of long life; so pine-crane paintings are often used as birthday gifts. Imperial buildings and courtyards are often decorated with statues of the "divine crane" as well as auspicious animals like the deer and the tortoise. Inside the Hall of Supreme Harmony in the Forbidden City, in front of the imperial throne and on either side, there is a bronze crane.

Elephants are auspicious animals.

Clay doll wearing a tiger-head cap and a pair of tiger-head shoes. Note the auspicious character 福 (pronounced as fu, meaning "happiness") on its chest.

In China, an affectionate couple is customarily referred to as "a pair of mandarin ducks". As the Chinese see it, mandarin ducks are the very embodiment of love, of mutual loyalty cherished by a couple. Indeed for its entire life a mandarin duck has only one mate of the opposite sex and, after one dies, the other will never "re-marry". Besides, the male and female birds in a pair are often seen "fondling" each other with their pecks, reminiscent of the husband and wife intoxicated with love. For that, male and female mandarin ducks in pairs are always a most popular theme of folk art, usually depicted in paintings decorating nuptial chambers and embroidered on wedding sheets and pillows.

In the Chinese language, the characters 鱼 (fish) and 余 (abundance) are homonyms, both pronounced as "yu". Because of this, fish is seen as a symbol of prosperity. Of fish of all species, the carp is most popular. In some parts of the country carps cooked in various ways are indispensable dishes for Spring Festival feasts. According to legend, in lunar March every year, carps will swim upstream the Yellow River, and the strongest few that throw themselves over the Dragon Arch in the turbulent waves midstream will instantly transform into dragons. In ancient times, scholars had the pet phrase "jumping over the Dragon Arch", meaning working hard in study in order to be successful in imperial examinations so that a poor scholar may rise to officialdom overnight. Fish spawns are countless. Believe it or not, in old times, a pair of jade fish was given to newlyweds as a gift in hope that they would produce many – if not countless — babies.

Harmony between Man and nature is an indispensable part of the Chinese culture, prompting the Chinese people to confine their feelings to plants and flowers and see them as embodiments of Man's virtue and other personal qualities. For their elegance and luxuriant beauty, peony is referred to as the "king of all flowers" and seen as the symbol of riches and honor. The pine and cypress are evergreen and always stand erect in defiance of wind and snow, thus symbolizing strength and willpower. In numerous poems and essays, people with an unyielding spirit, a will to defy evil under whatever circumstances, are compared to the pine and cypress. In old times, the pine and cypress were regarded as the noblest or the greatest of all plants. For that, these trees were planted round imperial mausoleums and tombs of high ministers. Ancient Chinese regarded the plum, orchid, chrysanthemum and bamboo as embodiments of high virtue, and often compared them to people of noble characters. The plum was accorded the honor because it ushers in Spring by opening its flowers that give forth a refreshing smell even though the weather is still cold. Though growing deep in forests where few people set foot in, the orchid quietly makes the world beautiful and pleasant with its fragrant flowers. The chrysanthemum blossoms after the Frost Descend, the 18th solar term, when other plants are withering. For that, it was used to refer to people who refused to associate with undesirable trends or practices. The bamboo is hollow inside and has joints which, in the eyes of ancient Chinese, symbolized modesty and moral integrity. The "four gentlemen of high virtue" have always been favorite themes of Chinese poetry and traditional Chinese paintings. By singing the praise of the "four gentlemen of high virtue" and portraying their images, poets and painters were actually expressing a kind of mental outlook, a pursuit of the highest moral attainment.

Fruits can also be seen as auspicious. In old times, pomegranate fruit was often used as a wedding gift because of the numerous enveloping seeds wrapped in its rind – again testifying to the old belief that more children means more happiness. Numerous legends and folk stories tell about "divine peach trees" growing in the Heavenly Garden, which blossom once in 3,000 years and bear fruit once in 5,000 years. Once a person has a bite of a "divine peach", the person will transform into an immortal. So at birthday parties for the aged, peaches or peach-shaped cakes are indispensable. Paintings or porcelain statues of the Longevity God, fairies and boy immortals with "divine" or "longevity peaches" in their hands are the most popular gifts to old people on their birthdays.

Auspicious Designs and Patterns

Knowledge of the decorative designs and patterns on traditional Chinese artifacts helps one understand the inner world of ancient Chinese and the country's folkways. Bronze wine vessels and food containers left over from the Shang-Zhou period, for example, often have relieves of a fierce-looking legendary animal called *tao tie* which, ancient Chinese believed, is greedy for food. The *tao tie* relieves were meant to tell those nobles and aristocrats who were using them not to be too extravagant in eating.

The inner world of the Chinese people manifests itself most strikingly in folk artworks like New Year paintings and paper cuts. New Year paintings originate from portraits of gods that ancient Chinese put up on their gates and doors on the Spring Festival supposedly to protect their families from invasion by evil spirits. As time went by, "door paintings" became diverse in theme as more and more people put up pictures expressing their aspirations or ideals for peace and wealth when important festivals were celebrated. The Ming-Qing period, in particular, saw a boom of door paintings with auspicious images or designs, which were put up not only for festivals but also on occasions like weddings, birthday parties for the aged, celebration of the first anniversary of a baby's birth and sacrificial ceremonies. The tradition of putting up folk paintings — generalized as "New Year paintings" — has been passed down to this day. There are paintings depicting men work the land while women do weaving, a scene typical of China's agricultural society. Also popular are paintings showing people celebrating a good harvest of crops, and paintings depicting families with people of several generations living happily under one roof or children performing filial duties to their parents or grandparents.

Emperor Qian Long (1736-1795) of the Qing Dynasty in full ceremonial dress.

A New Year painting on the traditional
theme "*qi lin* sending in babies".

In addition, not a few paintings are based on folk stories, legends and traditional operas, depicting their heroes and heroines or the most popular episodes in them. To sum up, New Year paintings, while important for their aesthetic and cultural value, carry strong massages as a tool of mass education.

Paper cuts are as popular as New Year paintings. Those on windows, known as *chuang hua*, are the most popular of all paper cuts as these are special for the Spring Festival. There are also paper cuts that are sent along with gifts or dowry — the so-called *xi hua* or "paper cuts of happiness". In the countryside, days before their weddings, a girl would busy cutting bright red paper into various auspicious designs special for the occasion — to show not only that she is nimble-figured but also her expectations of happiness and harmony in her new family. To the girl, these paper cuts are as important as her dowry or the "love pledge" to her future husband — usually a small, embroidered bag she has made by herself. There are paper cuts not for anything special, but even such paper cuts carry a message through those auspicious signs and patterns. Besides, paper cuts can be used as models for embroidery.

In Pursuit of Happiness and Good Luck

More than 2,000 years ago, the Chinese already specified the meanig of happiness-long life, wealth, peace, virtue and a natural death after a meaningful life. The connotation of happiness underwent changes in the later centuries, as manifested in more recent sayings such as "longevity, riches and honor make up for happiness" and "happiness means freedom from misfortune". At any rate, happiness, long life and many children in particular became the most popular pursuit.

The Chinese have always been family conscious. In old times, families of several generations living in complete harmony under one roof represented their highest pursuit, hence the saying "more children, more happiness". Traditional weddings invariably center on blessings on the couple to live in conjugal bliss to a ripe old age and to produce many children. Such blessings, so to speak, are "materialized" in those

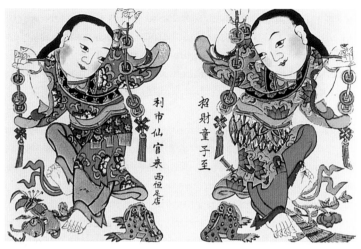

Wealth Gathering Deity and Market God
as depicted in a New Year painting.

wedding rituals and articles special for the occasion. When stepping
into the nuptial chamber, the bridegroom and bride hold either end of
a red silk ribbon with a heart-shaped bundle hanging from the middle,
suggesting that the couple are resolved to share each other's weal and
woe forever. The bridegroom and bride then will each cut off a tuft of
hair and weave the two tufts into a bundle, suggesting that from now
on they will be chained together as an officially married couple. Peony
flowers are often embroidered on the pillows and sheets on the nuptial
bed along with a white-crested bird. The peony flowers, symbolize
riches and honor and the white-crested bird, the hope that the couple
will love each other until their hair turns white. On the wall facing
south in the nuptial chamber there is a colorful painting depicting two
boy deities, one holding a lotus flower and the other, a round box. In
the Chinese language, the characters 荷 (lotus flower), 合 (box) and
和 (harmony) have the same pronunciation. So the painting embodies
a hope that the couple will live in "double" or even "triple" harmony.
In old times, the belief "more children, more happiness" would find
an even stronger expression at weddings. Before the bridegroom and
bride retired for the night, for example, well wishers would empty

baskets of dates, peanuts, lotus seeds, longans and nuts onto the nuptial bed, in hope that they would produce a baby early and that they would eventually have many children and grandchildren. The names of these fruits all have the same character 子, which also means "son". Moreover, the characters 枣 (dates) and 早 (early) are homonyms (pronounced as "zao"), and so are the characters 栗子 (nuts) and 立子 (give birth to a son), hence the connotation "give birth to a son early". In today's China, the old belief "more children, more happiness" has largely been abandoned and in cities, Western-style weddings are increasingly favored. In some remote, outlying rural areas, however, traditional weddings can still be seen.

The Chinese attach a great importance to life and regard respect of the aged as a highest virtue, and take many things as symbols of long life. Legends about immortals giving people long life have been passed down orally or in writing since remote antiquity. The God of Longevity, who is pictured as a smiling old man with an extruding forehead and a large "longevity peach" in his hand, has always been everybody's friend. Besides, the Chinese character 寿 (longevity) assume countless calligraphic styles, written or

Auspicious signs on a window.

printed either as an individual character or as part of an auspicious design on birthday gifts. Families have always paid great attention to celebrating birthdays of their elders. Birthday parties for the elderly can be simple or elaborate, depending on families' financial status. But the same rituals were followed at all such parties. The main room in the family's house, that is, the room facing south, will be decorated as the venue for the celebrations, with a large vertical streamer bearing the character 寿 displayed on the wall. Flanking the streamer is a couplet, reading "felicity overflowing like the endless torrents of the East Sea; life eternal like the divine pine on the South Mountain". The person having his or her birthday celebrated sits beside a table below the streamer to receive greetings, while the room is bright with red candles burning on the table. As a rule, there will be a birthday feast for all attending the party. The guests always bring with them gifts,

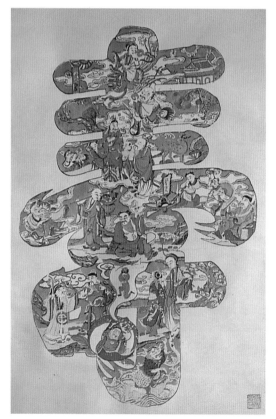

The character 寿 (pronounced as "shou", meaning longevity), formed with designs of immortals, pine trees, cranes and peaches that are all symbols of longevity.

A New Year painting — the fish and lotus flowers symbolizing abundance or prosperity.

the most popular of which are "longevity peaches", pieces of silk with the character 寿 written or embroidered on them, and couplets with complimentary words or greetings. In ancient times, birthday parties for persons of 60 years in age or older were referred to as 做寿 ("longevity-making parties"). This can probably be attributed to the fact that life expectancy in ancient times was much shorter than now and few could live that long, hence the special attention paid to birthday parties for people that old.

The Chinese characters play a unique role in helping people express their longings for happiness and good luck. The characters 福 (happiness) and 蝠 (bat) are homonyms, both pronounced as "fu". Just for that, bats are seen as auspicious animals. The deer symbolizes wealth because the character 鹿 (deer) is pronounced the same way as 禄, which means "official's salaries" or "wealth". On the Spring Festival, pieces of bright red paper with the character 福 (happiness) written on them are put up everywhere in a house — on walls, window and furniture. It may be interesting to note that sometimes, the pieces are deliberately put up upside down. The characters 倒 (upside down) and 到 (arrive) are homonyms, both pronounced as "dao". So families would be happy if somebody points out the "mistake" by saying "福倒了" (the character 福 is upside down), which sounds exactly like "福到了 (happiness arrives). In celebrating weddings, people will put up pieces of bright red paper with the character 喜喜 written on them. The character 喜 means "happiness" or a "happy event". This combination of two 喜characters suggests that the wedding is a happy event for the families of both the bridegroom and the bride.

Auspicious words like 福 and 喜 are always written on paper bright red in color, and so are those festival couplets. Besides, bright red lanterns are hung when happy events are celebrated. Bright red is, in fact, the color of happiness, the dominant color at weddings, birthday parties, festival gatherings, inauguration ceremonies, etc. In ancient times, it was the color special for aristocrats and ranking officials, hence the reference *zhu men* (bright red gate) to residences of upper class families, families that are rich and powerful. Here are two lines of a poem by Du Fu, a Tang Dynasty poet, which protests against inequality between the rich and the poor:

Wine and meat rot behind red gates
While frozen bodies by the roadside lie.

The yellow color is also seen as auspicious. In old times, however, it was the color for emperors and imperial families. The "dragon robes", some of which we still can see, are embroidered with gold yellow dragon designs. The roofs of imperial structures are invariably of glazed yellow tiles.

Modern Chinese are still family bound and attach much importance to blood lineage. But, as has been mentioned, few still cling to the old belief "more children, more happiness". Those traditional auspicious signals – signs, patterns, etc. – are still used to add beauty to people's life, but are losing or changing their folklorist implications. The Chinese people are developing a new way of life. Traditional festivals are still celebrated by hanging up red lanterns and colorful streamers and buntings. Nevertheless, festival activities are becoming increasingly diverse in form and variety. Calligraphy is appreciated as ever, but increasingly great numbers of people are writing on computers. Tea drinking remains a part of the Chinese culture. Meanwhile, coffer is consumed in increasing quantities. Traditional operas still have a large audience, but purely Western arts – ballet, symphonic music, for example – are becoming increasingly popular. Never have the Chinese people enjoyed so much freedom in deciding how to spend their lives and in choosing the color or colors that they think suit their tastes. The Chinese culture is developing, melting into modernity while retaining its originality. The Chinese will remain Chinese by nature. Erasable is the imprint of China's traditional culture in the souls of the Chinese — wherever they are, in China or outside.